To kristine +
Fan
Publix Cooking School

MY MODERN
AMERICAN TABLE

MY MODERN AMERICAN TABLE

—

Recipes for Inspired Home Cooks

—

SHAUN O'NEALE

EDITED BY LEDA SCHEINTAUB
PHOTOGRAPHY BY ANDREW PURCELL

Abrams, New York

Published in 2017 by Abrams, an imprint of ABRAMS.

MasterChef is a trademark of Shine Television, LLC and used under license.
The MasterChef logo is a trademark of Shine Limited and used under license.
All rights reserved. MasterChef is based on a format created by Franc Roddam
in association with Ziji Productions.

Library of Congress Control Number: 2016955656

ISBN: 978-1-4197-2400-8

Editor: Holly Dolce
Designer: Danielle Young
Production Manager: Anet Sirná-Bruder

Printed and bound in the United States
10 9 8 7 6 5 4 3 2 1

Abrams books are available at special discounts when purchased in quantity
for premiums and promotions as well as fundraising or educational use.
Special editions can also be created to specification. For details, contact
specialsales@abramsbooks.com or the address below.

ABRAMS The Art of Books
115 West 18th Street, New York, NY 10011
abramsbooks.com

Dedicated to the memory of my father,
Ronald K. Thalman, and to my mom

CONTENTS

Foreword

by **Gordon Ramsay**

When I learned we were going to have a Las Vegas DJ in the running for *MasterChef Season 7* I wasn't quite sure what to expect. Of course, Vegas DJs are known for entertaining, but for me that meant spinning the decks in glamorous clubs, not dishing out food across the dinner table. But from day one in the *MasterChef* Kitchen, Shaun O'Neale grabbed my attention with his culinary knowledge, boundless enthusiasm, and genuine passion for cooking. In challenge after challenge he demonstrated his deep love and understanding of food.

The beauty of this book is that Shaun has adapted his more complex recipes so that even novice home cooks can have fun making his dishes in their own kitchens. You'll be able to recreate and taste Shaun's delicious Bourbon-Braised Short Rib Ravioli, his Salted Caramel–Chocolate Tarts with Berry Sorbet, and his incredible woodland-inspired Ancho and Coffee–Rubbed Venison that really put him above the rest for his *MasterChef* win.

Shaun is so excited to have the opportunity to share his unique recipes and creative ideas for presentation with home cooks around the globe, and I couldn't be more proud. Shaun has had an amazing journey to become America's latest MasterChef, now it's your time to get cooking!

Lots of love,
Gordon

Introduction

My culinary journey doesn't start from a specific cultural heritage or family food tradition. It starts as a kid with a nerdy obsession for two things: music and food. Without a mentor, I taught myself about DJing and discovered my own personal style. The same goes with food—sure, we had turkey on Thanksgiving and made burgers on the Fourth of July, but without really being tied to specific flavors or cuisines, I eventually would find my way around the kitchen on my own.

Growing up, I was heavily involved in sports: I was an All-Conference soccer player, a pretty good basketball player, a defensive shortstop, and a Junior Olympic track and field athlete specializing in the javelin. Sports took me traveling around the country, and every time we would land in a new place, the first thing I wanted to do was go out for an amazing meal. From the restaurant at the top of the Space Needle in Seattle to the most amazing steakhouse in Houston to life-changing Creole food in New Orleans, my parents were always happy to join me on my food adventures. Maybe that is my family's culinary tradition!

When I turned seventeen, I was still competing in sports, but something new came into my life: electronic music and DJ culture. I was immediately hooked on the music and the control the DJ had over the crowd. It was like watching an orchestra conductor, but instead of musicians the DJ was orchestrating the dance floor, reshaping the energy of the room with every new song. Ultimately, the tie between music and food—all that mixing and blending and creating something new from scratch—was what pulled me into the kitchen.

Moving to Las Vegas turned out to be the best decision I could make, both for my career as a DJ and for expanding my culinary horizons. I have had the opportunity to perform at some of the most legendary nightclubs on the planet and have worked for Playboy, DreamWorks, and other top companies. My career culminated in the gig of a lifetime on New Year's Eve 2011, but sadly the most tragic moment of my life would come at the same time.

I was asked to perform outside Caesars Palace that New Year's Eve in front of more than one hundred thousand people. Just as I was about to say yes, on December 2, I got the call that my father was no longer with us. I had just spent Thanksgiving in Iowa with him, and although he had been very sick with COPD (Chronic Obstructive Pulmonary Disease), during that last visit he seemed to be better. Maybe subconsciously he knew what was coming and he wanted those last days to be about life and not fear of death. That Thanksgiving, I cooked my father the best prime rib I have ever made, and in this book I share the recipe as a celebration of his life. I wasn't sure if I could go on with the Caesars Palace event, but after a few sleepless nights I knew my dad would have wanted me in front of that crowd. So the show went on. It was the best set I had ever played, capped off with the first stage dive and crowd surfing ever seen on Las Vegas Boulevard. My father was only fifty-nine years old, and with his loss it really hit me how fragile and fleeting life is. After the event, I went on to work for the biggest nightlife companies in Vegas and around the world. I hope I have made you proud, Dad!

With all that Vegas has offered me as a DJ, none of it compares to the influence the city has had on my outlook on food. Amazing food is everywhere in Las Vegas! From the celebrity chefs on the Strip to Chinatown and the sushi place a minute from my house, Vegas is quickly becoming a culinary capital and a reflection of the diversity of cuisine in America today. Restaurants here are on the cutting edge, modernist cooking techniques are featured on high-end menus, and the many Asian and Latin American markets give us access to many off-the-wall ingredients.

Vegas is where I began to experiment with new techniques and ingredients. I would come home after a dinner out and research how to replicate the meal I'd just eaten, and this led to my interest in modernist cooking techniques. Also known as molecular gastronomy, modernist cuisine blends science and food to create new flavor and texture experiences, bringing the science lab into the kitchen.

Once I had the honor of DJing an event where Chef Richard Blais was giving a cooking demo. I was able to chat with him, and he gave me a copy of his book, *Try This at Home*. It was a game-changing moment for me. I must have cooked every single recipe in that book twice, and Chef Blais's influence can be seen in some of my recipes, such as the Crispy Pork Belly with Amaretto–Butternut Squash Puree (page 118).

Although modernist cooking has become my culinary backbone, I have always been obsessed with Italian culture, cuisine, and history. In 2013, I finally had an opportunity to see this breathtaking land for myself. There I found simplicity, extreme focus on the freshest in-season ingredients, and creativity with a respect for tradition. In Italy, everyone eats and drinks well no matter what their position in life, and the Italian passion for food oozes from every part of the peninsula. I brought that Italian frame of mind home to my kitchen, and it changed the way I cook forever.

Using modernist techniques while respecting tradition is something that has become very important to me. I am always forging ahead and creating new flavor combinations, and my unique style of plating sets the presentation of my food apart. Finding a balance between old and new can be challenging, but that is what makes it fun to me. I am no longer afraid or embarrassed to make mistakes in the kitchen. The greatest chefs on the planet constantly make mistakes while creating new dishes and flavor combinations!

This book is not your average home cook's cookbook. With it, I hope to inspire you to try new things to push your own boundaries and to never say that something is too complicated. I encourage you to use this book as a starting point in your culinary journey, because the secrets in these pages are what won me the *MasterChef Season 7* title.

Shaun O'Neale

MY MODERN AMERICAN KITCHEN

My take on modern American cuisine is experimental. It's edgy, it's international, it's made from scratch, and above all, it's fresh! That said, the first time you try the recipes, you'll be most successful when you follow them closely, but the second time through, experiment with new flavor combinations, use a technique from a meat dish for a dessert dish, or do something wild like adding lemon beurre blanc to a whipping siphon to make a foam. Cook with love, have fun in the kitchen, and you can't go wrong. You may burn a few things along the way, but that's part of the excitement!

My career as a DJ has put me on the cutting edge of technology and culture, which is why modernist cuisine, aka molecular gastronomy, absolutely fascinates me. Being able to compress a piece of melon or make ravioli with a see-through wrapper is mind-blowing. But don't be put off by the recipes with modernist components, like the venison dish I made for the *MasterChef* Finale that involves cherry smoking chips, a glass *cloche*, and an electric smoking gun! The recipes are just as

delicious without them, but when made with them they become something extra special. I find that half of the fun in food is exploration of the unknown, and I am always seeking out spices unfamiliar to me or a type of produce I have never seen before. So if something in this book is brand new to you, I urge you to you give it a try. Taste adventures can open you up to whole new worlds of food, so throw on an apron, dig in to the unfamiliar, and be prepared to be blown away!

Creating beautiful plates to match my big, bold, in-your-face flavors is something I take great pride in. The most important thing about plating is never to focus on it first! Always, and I mean always, develop the flavors of each component of a dish, and then take the time to process how those components should look on the plate. Save a few moments to create art on your plate; doing so will instantly elevate your dining experience. The photos show you how I plate my dishes, but they are just suggestions, and the recipes will be just as tasty whether plated for a date or served up family style.

Must-Have Ingredients *and* Go-To Recipes

SALT

My preference for salt is Maldon sea salt. Maldon salt is a gift to all cooks, as it adds so much flavor to anything it touches and little crispy, salty bites when used as a garnish. If you aren't familiar with Maldon, I implore you to seek it out; it is easily available online, in specialty food stores, and even in the salt section of some supermarkets. When you see "salt" in my recipes, either Maldon salt or kosher salt should be used. I've specifically indicated Maldon sea salt in recipes where it's particularly important to use it.

FATS

When it comes to olive oil, I tend to stick to middle-of-the-road quality for cooking and keep the fancy stuff to drizzle over completed dishes or for finishing salads and risottos. For frying oil, it's peanut oil, always!

With butter, I always use the best-quality unsalted butter I can find at my local grocery store.

DRIED CHILES

Dried chiles are a very important part of my cooking. They impart smoky, spicy, and even sweet flavors into all kinds of dishes. And when you toast the chiles first, you release their oils, and that means more flavors and aromas will be released into whatever you are cooking. For something that has such a big impact on flavor, it's a simple technique that takes very little time. From the smokiness of the ancho chile, to the heat of the árbol chile, to the beautiful sweetness of the guajillo chile, they are all essential in my cooking. All

of these chiles can be found in Latin American markets and online.

To toast dried chiles, heat a skillet over medium-high heat. Add your dried chiles and toast, shaking the pan constantly and turning the chiles a few times, for 2 to 5 minutes to release the oils in the chiles, until they are darkened in color but not burnt. Remove the chiles from the skillet and use as instructed in your recipe.

GARNISHES

My favorite plating garnishes are microgreens, as not only do they look beautiful on a plate; they also bring a great freshness to any dish. Micro arugula is peppery and crisp, while radish microgreens concentrate the flavor of a radish into a tiny green. As microgreens can be difficult to find, baby arugula can be substituted in most places for micro arugula and paper-thin radish slices can be used in place of the micro radish greens. Or it can be as easy as swapping in the best pieces of parsley or cilantro of the bunch or the nicest pieces of your carrot tops.

Roasted Garlic

The smell of garlic constantly permeates my home. Some call it my trademark scent, and that would be pretty accurate. The sweetness that comes out of garlic when roasted is unbelievable, with only subtle garlic undertones remaining, which means you can use a lot of it in your recipes. I use roasted garlic in my flavored butters for steak and seafood, to give depth to my All-Day Red Sauce (page 62), as

a base for my Roasted Garlic and Mushroom Risotto (page 74), in a marinade for steak and pork chops, and to make my Roasted Garlic Salt (see below). Sometimes I'll even munch on a roasted clove as a snack! Try substituting roasted garlic for fresh in some of your recipes and I promise you will be blown away by the results. I like to save the oil remaining on the aluminum foil to dip a slice of bread in.

MAKES 3 HEADS

3   heads garlic

1   tablespoon extra-virgin olive oil

Large pinch each salt and freshly ground
    black pepper

1   sprig fresh rosemary

1   sprig fresh thyme

Preheat the oven to 325°F (165°C).

Cut the top off each head of garlic, slightly exposing the cloves and keeping the head intact. Place the heads on a sheet of aluminum foil large enough to completely wrap all of them. Drizzle with the oil, sprinkle with the salt and pepper, top with the herbs, and seal the foil. Place the packet on a baking sheet and roast for 45 minutes to 1 hour, until the cloves are completely softened and lightly colored. Remove from the oven, cool, and store in an airtight container in the refrigerator for up to 1 week (store the garlic bulbs whole and squeeze the cloves out from the skins as you're ready to use them).

Roasted Garlic Salt

This addictive flavored salt has become a much-requested gift around the holidays. You can use it in place of regular salt in almost any savory recipe in this book or from your family's vault. After you get the garlic salt down, try other flavors: A favorite of mine is a sriracha-flavored salt that I use with my Asian-inspired dishes.

MAKES ABOUT 1 CUP (150 G)

2   heads Roasted Garlic (see opposite)

1   cup (120 g) Maldon sea salt or kosher salt

Set the oven to the lowest possible setting (mine is 170°F/70°C, but up to 200°F/90°C would still be fine).

Squeeze the roasted garlic out of the skins into a small food processor. Add ¼ cup (60 ml) water and process until smooth. Add the salt and pulse to incorporate.

Line a baking sheet with parchment paper and spread the salt mixture over it in an even layer. Bake it for 1½ to 2 hours, depending on how hot your oven is, stirring about halfway through, until the salt is completely dried out. Return the salt to the food processor and pulse to break it into granules about the size of kosher salt. Store in an airtight container in the pantry for up to 3 months.

Note: To get in some extra flavor, throw some fresh rosemary and thyme in with the salt while it bakes, or get creative and try some dried chiles or lemon peel.

COMPOUND BUTTERS

As a DJ, I am constantly on the lookout for new tricks to apply to my sets, with the sole purpose of exciting the dance floor. My feelings about flavored butters, known as "compound butters" in restaurant kitchens, are very similar. Basting seared meat in a beautiful compound butter gives your meal that extra high-end-restaurant edge. I could go on and on about the combinations I have come up with, like lavender-honey butter, perfect on fresh biscuits; or rosemary, orange, and chile butter, great for basting pork or chicken. For this book, though, I'm focusing on my three all-time favorites, the ones I use the most often—Roasted Garlic–Rosemary Butter, Chile-Lime Butter, and my all-time favorite, Foie Gras Steak Butter!

Roasted Garlic–Rosemary Butter

This is the compound butter I go to most often. I smear it over sourdough toasts and the bone marrow in my Roasted Bone Marrow recipe (page 36), and it is perfect for basting beef, pork, and chicken.

MAKES ABOUT 1½ CUPS (340 G)

2   heads Roasted Garlic (pages 16–17)

2   sticks (8 ounces/225 g) unsalted butter, at room temperature

1   tablespoon finely chopped fresh rosemary

1   teaspoon grated lemon zest

Large pinch each salt and freshly ground black pepper

Squeeze the roasted garlic out of the skins into a food processor and combine with the other ingredients. Process until thoroughly combined, stopping to scrape the sides of the machine as needed.

Scrape the butter onto a sheet of plastic wrap or parchment paper and tightly wrap it into a cylinder. The butter will keep for up to 2 weeks in the refrigerator or up to 2 months in the freezer.

Chile-Lime Butter

This butter is absolutely amazing with seafood. I feature it in my Chile and Lime Scallops recipe (page 27) and it is delicious with flaky fish such as halibut, sole, or grouper.

MAKES ABOUT 1½ CUPS (340 G)

2   dried ancho chiles, toasted (see page 16), stems and seeds removed, and torn into pieces

2   dried árbol chiles, toasted (see page 16), stems and seeds removed, and torn into pieces

½   jalapeño chile, finely diced

2   canned chipotle chiles in adobo sauce, chopped

2   sticks (8 ounces/225 g) unsalted butter, at room temperature

2   limes, zested and juiced

Large pinch each salt and freshly ground black pepper

Place the ancho and árbol chiles in a small food processor or spice grinder and process until broken down. Add the remaining ingredients and process until thoroughly combined.

Scrape the butter onto a sheet of plastic wrap or parchment paper and tightly wrap it into a cylinder. The butter will keep for up to 2 weeks in the refrigerator or up to 2 months in the freezer.

Foie Gras Steak Butter

This is my absolute favorite flavored butter. As you will see in the pages that follow, I love foie gras, and I can't make a steak in my house without foie butter for basting!

MAKES ABOUT 1½ CUPS (450 G)

8   ounces (225 g) foie gras, cut into roughly 1-inch (2.5-cm) cubes

2   sticks (8 ounces/225 g) unsalted butter, at room temperature

Huge pinch each salt and coarsely ground black pepper

Place all the ingredients in a food processor and process until thoroughly combined.

Scrape the butter onto a sheet of plastic wrap or parchment paper and tightly wrap it into a cylinder. The butter will keep for up to 4 days in the refrigerator or up to 2 months in the freezer.

ROASTED PEPPERS

Roasting brings out the flavor in bell peppers and tames the heat in poblanos and jalapeños. Roasted peppers play a big role in my cooking, from The Lees' Favorite Chili (page 126) to my Crispy Garlic Clams (page 30) and Sweet Corn with Roasted Chiles and Queso Fresco (page 150). Below are instructions for roasting peppers in the oven as well as a simpler open-flame method.

Oven-Roasted Red Bell Peppers or Chiles

Red bell peppers, poblano chiles, or jalapeño chiles (as many as you like)

Olive oil

Salt and freshly ground black pepper

Preheat the oven to 450°F (230°C).

Lightly coat your peppers in oil, season with salt and pepper, place on a roasting pan, and roast, turning them a couple times, until the skins are blistered and starting to turn black, about 50 minutes.

Place the peppers in a bowl and cover it with plastic wrap until they are cool enough to handle, about 15 minutes. Use your hands to remove the skins and seeds, and use the pepper flesh as directed in your recipe. Store in an airtight container in the refrigerator for up to 1 week.

Stovetop Roasted Red Bell Peppers or Chiles

Red bell peppers, poblano chiles, or jalapeño chiles (as many as your burners will fit)

Place your peppers over an open flame on your stovetop burners and char the peppers until the skin is black, turning them with tongs to get at all sides and being careful not to burn the flesh.

Place the peppers in a bowl and cover it with plastic wrap until they are cool enough to handle, about 15 minutes. Use your hands to remove the skins and seeds, and use the pepper flesh as directed in your recipe. Store in an airtight container in the refrigerator for up to 1 week.

STOCK

In my opinion, stock is the most important tool in both the professional and home kitchen. Stock is the starting point for so many incredible creations, most importantly sauces, but let's not forget soups and braises. I use stock to cook vegetables and potatoes, and I sub it for water in a lot of my recipes. Why not take the opportunity to impart some extra flavor whenever you can?

I strongly suggest you make your own stock at home. It's much simpler than you may think—just save all your scraps! By scraps I mean any leftover poultry carcasses or steak bones; throw them in a freezer bag and save them up in the freezer. Then when you're chopping vegetables, save your carrot peelings, celery ends, onion skins, and roots and pull them out anytime to make an amazing vegetable stock. Most recipes will instruct you to simmer your stock for hours and hours, but I have simplified mine by cooking it over high heat to reduce it and really concentrate the flavors. Making stock at home gives you the opportunity to control the flavor and salt level of your finished stock, which in turn adds just the right punch of flavor in the final dish. And it will save you money, too!

Vegetable Stock

MAKES ABOUT 2 QUARTS (2 L)

2   tablespoons olive oil

2   carrots, roughly chopped

2   onions, roughly chopped

2   stalks celery, including leaves, roughly chopped

1   green bell pepper, roughly chopped

1   red bell pepper, roughly chopped

1   jalapeño chile, cut in half and seeds removed

1   head garlic, cloves smashed

Salt and freshly ground black pepper

2   sprigs fresh thyme

1   bay leaf

In the biggest pot you own, heat the oil over medium-high heat. Add the carrots, onions, celery, bell peppers, jalapeño, and garlic. Season with salt and pepper and cook, stirring frequently, until the vegetables take on some color, about 10 minutes. (If you can't fit everything in at once, add the oil and vegetables in two batches, removing each to a bowl as they are finished.) Add 1 gallon (3.8 L) water, the thyme, and bay leaf and season with salt. Increase the heat to high, bring to a boil, and boil until reduced by half, about 1 hour. Strain the stock into a large bowl, pressing on the solids to extract all the liquid, and let cool.

Pour the stock into containers. It will keep for up to 1 week in the refrigerator or in the freezer (making sure to leave room for expansion so your container doesn't explode) for up to 6 months.

Beef Stock

MAKES ABOUT 2 QUARTS (2 L)

2   tablespoons olive oil
1   pound (455 g) marrow bones
1   pound (455 g) beef bones (ask your butcher for them)
8   ounces (225 g) lean ground beef
1   onion, roughly chopped
1   carrot, roughly chopped
1   stalk celery, roughly chopped
6   cloves garlic, smashed
Salt and freshly ground black pepper
2   sprigs fresh thyme
1   bay leaf

In the biggest pot you own, heat the oil over medium-high heat. Add the bones and cook, turning a few times, until colored all over. Remove the bones to a bowl. Add the ground beef and cook, stirring often to break it up, until browned and cooked through, about 10 minutes. Remove the beef to a strainer to

drain off excess fat and add the onion, carrot, celery, and garlic to the pot. Season with salt and pepper and cook, stirring frequently, until the vegetables take on some color, about 10 minutes. Return the bones and ground beef to the pan, add 1 gallon (3.8 L) water, the thyme, and bay leaf, and season with salt. Increase the heat to high, bring to a boil, and boil until reduced by half, about 1 hour. Reduce the heat to medium-low and cook at a bare simmer for 1 hour more (you could go for another hour to further concentrate the flavors if you like). Strain the stock into a large bowl, pressing on the solids to extract all the liquid, and let cool.

Skim the fat off the top of the stock and pour the stock into containers. It will keep for about 1 week in the refrigerator or in the freezer (making sure to leave room for expansion so your container doesn't explode) for up to 6 months.

Chicken Stock

MAKES ABOUT 2 QUARTS (2 L)

2   tablespoons olive oil
2   pounds bone-in chicken legs and thighs
Salt and freshly ground black pepper
2   onions, roughly chopped
2   carrots, roughly chopped
2   stalks celery, roughly chopped
4   cloves garlic, smashed
2   sprigs fresh thyme
1   bay leaf

In the biggest pot you own, heat the oil over medium-high heat. Add the chicken legs and thighs, season with salt and pepper, and cook for about 5 minutes without turning them (this allows the fat to render so the chicken doesn't stick to the pan). Cook until lightly browned, then turn and cook for another 3 to 5 minutes to lightly brown the second side. Remove the chicken to a bowl. Add the onions, carrots, celery, and garlic to the pot, season with salt and pepper, and cook, stirring frequently, until the vegetables take on some color, about 10 minutes. Return the chicken legs and thighs to the pan, add 1 gallon (3.8 L) water, the thyme, and bay leaf, and season with salt. Increase the heat to high, bring to a boil, and boil until reduced by half, about 1 hour. Reduce the heat to medium-low and cook at a bare simmer for 1 hour more. Strain the stock into a large bowl, pressing on the solids to extract all the liquid, and let cool.

Skim the fat off the top of the stock and pour the stock into containers. It will keep for up to 1 week in the refrigerator or in the freezer (making sure to leave room for expansion so your container doesn't explode) for up to 6 months.

Strain the stock into a large bowl, pressing on the solids to extract all the liquid, and let cool.

Pour the stock into containers. It will keep for up to 1 week in the refrigerator or in the freezer (making sure to leave room for expansion so your container doesn't explode) for up to 6 months.

Shellfish Stock

MAKES ABOUT 2 QUARTS (2 L)

2   tablespoons olive oil

Shells from 3 pounds (1.4 kg) shrimp, crab, or a mix of shellfish

Salt and freshly ground black pepper

2   carrots, roughly chopped

2   stalks celery, roughly chopped

In the biggest pot you own, heat 1 tablespoon of the oil over medium-high heat. Add the shells, season with salt and pepper, and cook, stirring frequently, until the shells are lightly colored all over, about 5 minutes. Remove the shells to a bowl. Add the remaining 1 tablespoon oil to the pan, reduce the heat to medium, then add the carrots and celery. Season with salt and pepper and cook, stirring frequently, until the vegetables start to soften, about 5 minutes. Return the shells to the pan, add 1 gallon (3.8 L) water, and season with salt. Increase the heat to high, bring to a boil, and boil until reduced by half, about 1 hour.

SMALL PLATES

The American small plates explosion comes as no surprise to me, as small-plate eating has been the norm in bars around the globe for hundreds of years, from tapas in Spain to *cicchetti* in Venice. When I was in Venice, *cicchetti* (snacks) were pretty much all I ate, with the cost tallied by the number of toothpicks you have on your plate at the end. Needless to say, I'd end up with a large stack of toothpicks after a couple Negronis!

But small plates are more than a means of soaking up a few too many adult beverages. How many times have you placed your order and then saw another mouthwatering plate delivered to the next table? Small plates eliminate that problem completely—you can have it all! The recipes in this chapter are perfect for a cocktail party and some, like my Chile and Lime Scallops (page 27), can easily be made into a dinner just by adding more to the plate. My Roasted Bone Marrow (page 36) is one of the most popular with my friends, and I bet yours will enjoy it as well!

Hamachi Crudo

with Wasabi Aioli

When you're working with raw fish, it all comes down to quality. I happen to be lucky when it comes to sourcing fish, as my good buddy Ron, from The Butcher Block here in Las Vegas, goes out of his way to get me the best. I suggest you build a relationship with your fishmonger; be good to those who handle the fish and they will be good to you. For this crudo, I chose hamachi, also known as Pacific yellowtail tuna. If you are unable to find hamachi, another type of high-quality tuna can be swapped in.

Note that the aioli makes about 1½ cups (360 ml) and keeps for up to a week. You'll have plenty left over to use with my Seared Sesame Tuna with Quail Eggs (page 88), and it goes great on sandwiches in place of regular mayo. Ponzu sauce and yuzu juice can be found in Asian food markets, and ponzu sauce can be found in many supermarkets.

■■■■■■■➡ **SERVES 4** ◀■■■■■■

Prepare the hamachi: Using a very sharp slicing knife or chef's knife, cut the hamachi into ¼-inch- (6-mm-) thick slices. Place a piece of plastic wrap over a large cutting board. Set the slices on the plastic and top with another piece of plastic to cover. Using a meat mallet, pound the slices evenly until they are ⅛ inch (3 mm) thick.

Arrange the fish on a serving plate or platter that's at least 12 inches (30.5 cm) in diameter, filling in all gaps and leaving about ½ inch (12 mm) of space around the edges of the plate. Refrigerate the hamachi while you make the marinade.

Make the marinade: In a small bowl, whisk together the ponzu sauce, soy sauce, lime zest, lime juice, yuzu juice, and toasted sesame oil. Add the árbol chile and season

(recipe continues)

FOR THE HAMACHI AND MARINADE:

1   pound (455 g) fresh, sashimi-grade hamachi (Pacific yellowtail tuna)

2   tablespoons ponzu sauce

2   tablespoons soy sauce

1   teaspoon grated lime zest

2   tablespoons fresh lime juice

1   teaspoon yuzu juice or fresh lemon juice

1   teaspoon toasted sesame oil

1   dried árbol chile

Freshly ground black pepper

FOR THE WASABI AIOLI:

1   large egg

¼   cup (60 ml) rice vinegar

¼   cup (60 ml) mirin

2   shallots, roughly chopped

⅓   cup (75 ml) wasabi paste (if you don't like it spicy, cut back to ¼ cup)

1½ cups (360 ml) olive oil

Salt and freshly ground black pepper

GARNISHES

Very thinly sliced jalapeño chile

Very thinly sliced radish

Scallions, thinly sliced on a bias

Small fresh cilantro leaves

Togarashi spice blend (see Note)

with pepper. Cover and let it rest in the refrigerator for 30 minutes for the flavors to combine.

Make the wasabi aioli: While the marinade is in the refrigerator, fill a small bowl with ice and water to make an ice water bath. Bring a small pot of water to a boil over high heat and salt the water. Lower the egg into the water, reduce the heat to medium, cover, and cook for exactly 6 minutes. Remove the egg from the water and place it in the ice water bath. Let it cool completely, then peel it. In a small skillet, combine the vinegar, mirin, and shallots, place over medium-high heat, and cook until the liquid is reduced by two-thirds, about 5 minutes. Strain the liquid into a blender, discarding the shallots, and give it a couple of minutes to cool. Add the peeled egg and wasabi to the blender and blend to combine. With the motor on low, very slowly drizzle in the oil through the feed tube to thicken the aioli to a creamy consistency. Season with salt and pepper and transfer to a squeeze bottle for plating (if you don't have a squeeze bottle, use a small spoon to top the crudo with aioli).

Finish the hamachi: Remove the hamachi and marinade from the refrigerator. Lightly brush the hamachi with the marinade. Return the hamachi to the refrigerator and leave it for 10 minutes. Remove from the refrigerator and serve with the jalapeño, radish, and scallion slices scattered around the plate. Sprinkle with the cilantro leaves and dot with varying sizes of wasabi aioli squeezed from the squeeze bottle. Finish with a light sprinkle of togarashi powder and serve.

Note: *Togarashi* is a chile-based Japanese spice blend easily found at Asian markets and online.

Chile and Lime Scallops

with Cauliflower-Fennel Puree *and* Lemon-Caviar Vinaigrette

It wasn't that long ago that I wasn't a fan of scallops; whenever I had them at a restaurant, they were over-cooked and rubbery, and I had never really attempted to make them at home. Then an experience at a Vegas sushi restaurant completely changed my thinking. There, the chef prepared the scallops so lightly seared that they essentially were still raw, with the lightest yuzu and chile vinaigrette. Those scallops inspired this recipe, with my Chile-Lime Butter (page 18) adding a Southwestern smoky, citrusy burst of flavor that pairs perfectly with the briny caviar. We all know that caviar can be an expensive ingredient, so make this as a special-occasion recipe, or simply leave the caviar out for a weeknight meal.

━━━━▶ **SERVES 4** ◀━━━━

Make the cauliflower-fennel puree: Combine the milk and cream in a large saucepan, place over medium heat, and bring to a simmer. Season with salt. Add the cauliflower and fennel and return the liquid to a simmer. Reduce the heat to medium-low and cook, stirring occasionally, for 20 minutes, or until the vegetables are tender.

While the cauliflower and fennel are cooking, melt the butter in a small saucepan over medium heat and cook for about 8 minutes, until the butter has a nutty aroma and browned bits begin to form on the bottom of the pan. Watch the butter carefully, because it can quickly go from browned to burnt. Remove the browned butter from the heat and set it aside.

Strain the cauliflower and fennel through a medium-mesh strainer set over a bowl, reserving the liquid.

(recipe continues)

FOR THE CAULIFLOWER-FENNEL PUREE:

1½ cups (360 ml) whole milk

1½ cups (360 ml) heavy cream

Salt

½ medium head cauliflower, roughly chopped

1 large fennel bulb, cored and roughly chopped, fronds reserved for garnish

½ stick (2 ounces/55 g) unsalted butter

Freshly ground white pepper

FOR THE LEMON-CAVIAR VINAIGRETTE:

Grated zest of ½ lemon

¼ cup (60 ml) fresh lemon juice

1 tablespoon honey

1 teaspoon Dijon-style mustard

½ cup (120 ml) extra-virgin olive oil

1 ounce of your favorite caviar (I recommend a Beluga and Kaluga hybrid such as Sasanian Kaluga 000)

Salt

FOR THE GARNISHES:

2 tablespoons fresh or frozen peas

Pea Puree (page 90), slightly warmed

Fennel fronds

Pea tendrils

FOR THE SCALLOPS:

12 medium scallops

2 tablespoons extra-virgin olive oil

¼ cup (55 g) Chile-Lime Butter (page 18)

Transfer the cauliflower and fennel to a blender, add ½ cup (120 ml) of the reserved liquid, and blend on medium speed for 1 minute, then increase the speed to high and blend until pureed. Reduce the speed to medium, add the browned butter to the blender, and blend. Gradually increase the speed to high until you have a smooth and creamy puree that is able to hold a soft mound without collapsing. If the puree is too thick, add more liquid 1 teaspoon at a time until it is the right consistency. Season with salt and white pepper.

Make the vinaigrette: In a small bowl, whisk together the lemon zest, lemon juice, honey, and mustard. Slowly drizzle in the oil, whisking constantly until emulsified. Using a spoon, gently mix in the caviar and season with salt.

Blanch the peas: Fill a medium bowl with ice and water to make an ice water bath. Bring a medium pot of water to a boil and heavily salt it. Add the peas and blanch them for 2 minutes, then transfer them to the ice bath to cool. Drain, then pat dry with a paper towel.

Make the scallops: Rinse and clean the scallops under cold water and pat them dry with paper towels. Place the scallops on a plate and let them come to room temperature, about 10 minutes.

Heat a large cast-iron pan over high heat until smoking, then add the oil. Season the scallops with salt. Working around the pan like the hands of a clock, add the scallops to the pan starting at 12 o'clock. When all the scallops are in the pan, cook for 1 minute, or until lightly browned on the bottom, then use a metal spatula to flip the scallops, starting with the first one you placed at the 12 o'clock spot. When all the scallops have been flipped, add the chile-lime butter to the pan and turn off the heat. Using a spoon, baste the scallops for 2 minutes, or until they are cream colored and lightly browned on the second side and white and tender inside. (If the scallops overcook, they will become rubbery.) Immediately transfer the scallops from the skillet onto a large plate.

To plate: Spoon a medium circle of the cauliflower-fennel puree onto the center of each plate. Spoon the pea puree into a squeeze bottle and squeeze it over part of the cauliflower puree. Set three scallops per plate onto the puree, with one scallop leaning on the other two. Working in a straight line through the plate, squeeze about seven small dots of the pea puree across the plate, then place individual peas randomly along the same line. Slowly pour the caviar vinaigrette over the scallops, allowing the caviar to fall on top of the scallops. Finish with a sprinkling of fennel fronds and pea tendrils.

Crispy Garlic Clams

While filming *MasterChef* in Los Angeles, we had an opportunity to eat at an amazing seafood restaurant near our hotel. Their garlic clams—steamed, battered in their shells, fried, and covered in copious amounts of garlic—quickly became a group favorite and inspired this take on the dish. I didn't fry the clams because it's so easy to overcook them in a home kitchen; instead I fried the garlic to bring a great crunch to the dish. Serve the clams with some nice crusty bread to soak up all of those amazing juices.

➡ SERVES 4 ⬅

Make the fried garlic: Measure out 2 tablespoons of the minced garlic and set aside for cooking the clams. Drain the remaining minced garlic from the jar and spread it onto a paper towel–lined plate in an even layer. Place another paper towel on top of the garlic and allow it to sit for 20 minutes to remove as much moisture as possible.

While the garlic is sitting, heat the oil to 350°F (175°C) in a small saucepan over medium heat. Add the garlic to the oil and cook for about 1 minute, until golden brown, then pour the oil through a fine-mesh strainer into a bowl. Remove the garlic to a new paper towel–lined plate to dry and then season with salt. Reserve the garlic-infused oil to cook the clams and to use in place of plain oil in any savory recipe.

FOR THE FRIED GARLIC:

2   (4½-ounce/130-g) jars minced garlic

2   cups (480 ml) peanut oil

Salt

FOR THE STEAMED CLAMS:

1   large shallot, minced

Salt and freshly ground black pepper

¾   cup (180 ml) dry white wine, such as Pinot Grigio

¾   cup (180 ml) Chicken Stock (page 20)

1   teaspoon red pepper flakes

1   lemon, zested

2   lemons, juiced

2½ pounds (1.2 kg) Manila clams, cleaned

FOR THE GARNISHES:

Chopped fresh flat-leaf parsley

Grated lemon zest

Maldon sea salt

Cook the clams: In a large saucepan, heat 2 tablespoons of the reserved oil over medium-high heat. Add the shallot and cook for about 2 minutes, until lightly browned. Add the reserved 2 tablespoons garlic and cook for 2 minutes, or until lightly browned. Season with salt and pepper. Add the wine, stir to release any browned bits that stuck to the pan, and cook until reduced by half, about 5 minutes. Add the stock and red pepper flakes and reduce by half again, about 5 minutes. Add the lemon zest and juice and the clams and cover the pot. Cook for about 5 minutes, stirring a couple times, until the clams have opened, discarding any that don't open.

To serve: Using a slotted spoon, remove the clams from the cooking liquid to serving bowls. Spoon some of the broth into the bowls, sprinkle the garlic over the clams, and finish with a little parsley, lemon zest, and salt.

Bacon-Wrapped Stuffed Shrimp

Really, could it get any better? I have been making these shrimp for many years now, so this recipe has stood the test of time in my house. I serve them here with a very simple orange dipping sauce easily made from pantry items. Don't get frustrated wrapping the shrimp in bacon; it takes a few tries to get the hang of it, but by the end you will be a pro!

▶ SERVES 6 AS AN APPETIZER ◀
▶ MAKES 18 SHRIMP ◀

Make the stuffed shrimp: Preheat the oven to 425°F (220°C) and line a baking sheet with aluminum foil.

Using a sharp knife, gently cut down the back of each shrimp to open it up for the stuffing. You are essentially butterflying the shrimp without cutting all the way through. Place the shrimp on a plate and refrigerate until ready to stuff.

In a medium bowl, combine the crab, cream cheese, lemon zest, lemon juice, jalapeño, and cilantro and season with salt and pepper. Mix well to combine. Cover and refrigerate for 30 minutes to allow the mixture to tighten up.

Stuff each shrimp with about 1 tablespoon of the crab mixture and tightly wrap a bacon half around the shrimp. Repeat with the remaining crab mixture and shrimp. Place the shrimp with the seams facing down on the prepared baking sheet and bake for about 15 minutes, until the bacon starts to crisp. Turn the oven to broil and let it heat up. Place the pan on the top rack of the oven and broil for about 3 minutes on each side, until crisp all over.

FOR THE BACON-WRAPPED STUFFED SHRIMP:

- 18 large shrimp, peeled and deveined
- 8 ounces (225 g) jumbo lump crab, drained if needed
- 4 ounces (115 g) cream cheese, softened
- 1 teaspoon grated lemon zest
- 2 tablespoons fresh lemon juice
- 1 tablespoon minced jalapeño chile
- 1 tablespoon minced fresh cilantro
- Salt and freshly ground black pepper
- 9 slices bacon (about 1 pound/ 455 g), cut in half lengthwise

FOR THE ORANGE DIPPING SAUCE:

- ½ cup (120 ml) orange marmalade
- 1 tablespoon rice vinegar
- 1 tablespoon sambal oelek (chili-garlic paste; see Note)

Make the orange dipping sauce: While the shrimp are in the oven, in a small bowl, whisk together the marmalade, vinegar, and sambal oelek to combine.

To serve: Place the shrimp on a platter directly from the broiler and serve the dipping sauce on the side.

Note: *Sambal oelek* is a spicy chili paste very popular in Asian cuisines. It can be found in Asian food markets.

Crispy Confit Duck Leg Tacos

with Pickled Shallots, Mango Salsa, *and* Jalapeño Sauce

I first learned how to confit—a preservation method—when I was trying to use all of my garden's tomatoes. To take my confit skills a little further, I started working with duck legs. There is no better taco out there!

▶ **SERVES 4** ◀

Marinate the duck legs: In a small food processor, combine the ancho chile, árbol chile, peppercorns, thyme, rosemary, salt, and sugar and process until broken down. Rub the duck legs all over with the salt mixture, place in a zip-top or vacuum-seal bag, and refrigerate for at least 2 hours or up to overnight.

Confit the duck: Remove the duck legs from the refrigerator and bring them to room temperature. Melt the duck fat in a cast-iron Dutch oven or another heavy-bottomed saucepan just big enough to fit the legs. Add the thyme, ancho chile, and árbol chile. Place over medium-high heat and bring the fat to 200°F (90°C) on a frying thermometer attached to the side of the pan. Submerge the duck legs in the fat, leaving a bit of the salt and spices on the duck. Return the heat to 200°F (90°C), then reduce the heat to low and cook at a bare simmer for about 4 hours. Make sure the fat doesn't go above 200°F (90°C) while cooking, and cook until the meat browns, shrinks off the bone, and is very tender. Leave the duck legs to cool in the fat off the heat.

Make the pickled shallots: While the duck is cooking, place the pickling spice in a small saucepan and toast over medium-high heat for 5 minutes, or until aromatic. Add the red wine vinegar, apple cider vinegar, sugar,

FOR THE DUCK LEGS AND RUB:

1 dried ancho chile, toasted (see page 16), stemmed, seeded, and torn into pieces

1 dried árbol chile, toasted (see page 16), stemmed, seeded, and torn into pieces

20 black peppercorns, toasted

Leaves from 3 sprigs fresh thyme

Leaves from 1 sprig fresh rosemary

¼ cup (30 g) salt

2 tablespoons granulated sugar

4 skin-on duck legs

FOR THE CONFIT:

5 cups (1.2 L) duck fat

3 sprigs fresh thyme

1 dried ancho chile

1 dried árbol chile

FOR THE PICKLED SHALLOTS:

2 tablespoons pickling spice

½ cup (120 ml) red wine vinegar

¼ cup (60 ml) apple cider vinegar

¼ cup (50 g) granulated sugar

2 tablespoons salt

3 large shallots, thinly sliced

salt, and ½ cup (120 ml) water. Bring to a boil, and boil for 3 minutes. Place the shallots in a glass jar, strain the pickling mixture over the shallots, and leave them to pickle for at least 1 hour and up to 4 hours. Set aside for plating.

Make the mango salsa: In a medium bowl, combine the mango, onion, jalapeño, and garlic. In a small bowl, whisk together the champagne vinegar, oil, lime juice, and honey until the honey is dissolved. Add to the mango mixture and stir to fully coat. Set aside for 1 hour to allow the flavors to infuse. Stir in the cilantro and season with salt and pepper just before serving.

Make the jalapeño sauce: In a medium skillet, heat the oil over medium-low heat. Add the onion and jalapeño and cook, stirring often, for 15 minutes, or until the onions are translucent. Add the vinegar, increase the heat to medium-high, and cook for 2 minutes, or until it is absorbed. Add the stock, brown sugar, honey, salt, and pepper and cook for about 10 minutes, until reduced by half. Strain and discard the solids. Set the sauce aside.

Finish the duck: Carefully remove the duck from the fat (reserve the duck fat for any and all of your frying needs), pat off excess fat with paper towels, and place the duck legs on a plate. Heat a large cast-iron skillet over high heat until scorching hot. Add the duck legs and cook for about 3 minutes, until the skin is crisp. Place the duck legs on a wire rack to cool for 5 minutes. Remove the skin from the legs and return it to the skillet to crisp up the underside that was attached to the leg; return it to the wire rack for a couple of minutes, then chop it. Shred the meat from the duck legs so it resembles pulled pork. Stir the jalapeño sauce into the meat.

To serve: Line up your tortillas, duck confit, mango salsa, pickled shallots, and garnishes and serve them taco bar–style, topping your tacos with the crispy duck skin, crema, cilantro, micro arugula, and radish microgreens.

Note: Mexican crema is basically a cross between heavy cream and sour cream. In a pinch, you can use sour cream in its place.

FOR THE MANGO SALSA:

1 ripe mango, peeled and finely chopped

½ medium red onion, finely chopped

½ jalapeño chile, diced

2 cloves garlic, minced

1 tablespoon champagne vinegar or white wine vinegar

1 tablespoon extra-virgin olive oil

2 tablespoons fresh lime juice

1 tablespoon honey

¼ cup (10 g) chopped fresh cilantro

Salt and freshly ground black pepper

FOR THE JALAPEÑO SAUCE:

1 tablespoon extra-virgin olive oil

½ red onion, chopped

4 jalapeño chiles, seeded and chopped

¼ cup (60 ml) sherry vinegar

1 cup (240 ml) Chicken Stock (page 20)

¼ cup (55 g) packed brown sugar

1 tablespoon honey

Salt and freshly ground black pepper

About 12 small corn tortillas, heated

FOR THE GARNISHES:

Mexican crema (see Note)

Fresh cilantro leaves

Micro arugula

Radish microgreens

Roasted Bone Marrow

with Bourbon, Fig, and Bacon Jam and Sourdough Toasts

Bone marrow is on menus all over the place these days, and for good reason—it's damn delicious. Some people have even gone as far as to give it the moniker "God's butter." This is a recipe for bone marrow in its simplest form, roasted with sourdough toast, which I like to spread with Roasted Garlic–Rosemary Butter (page 18) and serve with a fresh fig jam. The jam is also great on A King's Slider (page 39), and if you have any left over, it's perfect simply slathered on some toast by itself. Fresh figs are best for this recipe, but if you are unable to find them, you may substitute dried figs.

I serve this dish family style on a large wooden cutting board with the bones stacked in the middle, the toasts stacked up on the side, and the jam in a Mason jar alongside.

➡ SERVES 4 ⬅

Prep the marrow: Preheat the oven to 400°F (205°C).

Place the marrow bones cut-side up on a baking sheet and sprinkle the salt over them. Allow the marrow to come to room temperature while the oven is preheating, about 30 minutes.

Make the bourbon, fig, and bacon jam: In a large, heavy-bottomed skillet, cook the bacon over medium-high heat until the fat is rendered and the bacon is almost crisp, about 8 minutes. Remove the bacon to a paper towel–lined plate, reserving the fat in the skillet. Add the onions, reduce the heat to medium, and cook,

(recipe continues)

FOR THE BONE MARROW:

4 (8-inch/20-cm or so) beef marrow bones, cut in half lengthwise by your butcher

2 tablespoons Maldon sea salt

3 tablespoons Roasted Garlic–Rosemary Butter (page 18), at room temperature

5 sprigs fresh thyme

5 sprigs fresh rosemary

6 cloves garlic, peeled

Freshly ground black pepper

FOR THE BOURBON, FIG, AND BACON JAM:

6 slices bacon, cut into lardons (¼-inch/6-mm widthwise strips)

2 small yellow onions, thinly sliced

12 fresh black figs, stemmed and chopped

1 cup (240 ml) bourbon

¼ cup (55 g) packed brown sugar

¼ cup (60 ml) honey

2 tablespoons fresh lemon juice

Salt and freshly ground black pepper

FOR THE SOURDOUGH TOASTS:

1 sourdough baguette

3 tablespoons Roasted Garlic–Rosemary Butter (page 18), at room temperature

stirring frequently, for about 15 minutes, until they start to caramelize. Return the lardons after 10 minutes. Add the figs and cook for 4 minutes, or until they begin to soften. Add the bourbon, brown sugar, and honey and cook at a simmer, stirring frequently, until the liquid is almost completely evaporated and the mixture has a thick jam consistency, about 20 minutes, adding a little water if the pan starts to dry at any time. Note that the jam will thicken as it cools, so be careful not to overcook it. Add the lemon juice, season with salt and pepper, and remove the jam to a bowl to cool.

Toast the bread: Cut the baguette into ½-inch- (12-mm-) thick slices (I like to cut them at an angle for a nice presentation). Spread each slice with some of the garlic-rosemary butter, place them on a baking sheet, and bake for 10 minutes, or until golden brown and crispy around the edges. Remove from the oven and set aside for plating.

Roast the marrow and serve: Spread the garlic-rosemary butter evenly over the marrow bones. Scatter the thyme, rosemary, and garlic over the marrow, season with pepper, and roast for 15 to 20 minutes, until lightly browned and slightly bubbling but not melted. Remove from the oven. To serve, spread the marrow on the toasts, followed by a slathering of jam.

A King's Slider:

Kobe, Foie Gras, *and* Apricot-Bacon Jam *with* Parsnip Chips

This is not your average bar slider: This is the slider to end all sliders. Foie gras is one of my favorite ingredients, and I use it anywhere I can, so it was a logical move to add it to a slider. The apricot-bacon jam adds an incredibly deep sweetness and, surprisingly, cuts through the fat of the foie gras. If you'd rather not use foie gras in your sliders, don't worry about it. The burger with the apricot jam is delicious, just not quite as decadent. You could call that a prince's slider!

SERVES 5

MAKES 15 SLIDERS

Make the jam: In a large, heavy-bottomed skillet, cook the bacon over medium-high heat until the fat is rendered and the bacon is almost crisp, about 8 minutes. Remove the bacon to a paper towel–lined plate, reserving the fat in the skillet. Add the onions, reduce the heat to medium, and cook. Stir frequently until they start to caramelize, about 15 minutes, returning the lardons after 10 minutes. Add the vinegar and sugar and cook for 3 minutes, or until the vinegar is mostly absorbed. Add the preserves and cook at a simmer for about 10 minutes, stirring frequently, adding a little water if the pan starts to dry, until the mixture resembles a thick jam. Note that the jam will thicken as it cools, so be careful not to overcook it. Add the lemon juice, season with salt and pepper, stir to combine, and remove to a bowl to cool.

Make the beef patties: Form the beef into fifteen patties (a little more than 2 ounces/55 g each), making a small indention with your thumb on the top of each patty (this reduces shrinkage as they cook), placing them on

(recipe continues)

FOR THE APRICOT-BACON JAM:

5   slices bacon, cut into lardons (¼-inch/6-mm widthwise strips)

2   small yellow onions, sliced as thinly as possible

2   tablespoons white wine vinegar

2   tablespoons granulated sugar

1   cup (240 ml) apricot preserves

2   tablespoons fresh lemon juice

Salt and freshly ground black pepper

FOR THE KOBE SLIDERS:

2   pounds (910 g) ground Kobe or Wagyu beef

15   mini pretzel buns

½   stick (2 ounces/55 g) unsalted butter, melted

Salt and freshly ground black pepper

Garlic powder

Onion powder

3   tablespoons extra-virgin olive oil

FOR THE FOIE GRAS:

1   pound (455 g) Grade A foie gras

Salt and freshly ground black pepper

FOR THE PARSNIP CHIPS:

4   cups (960 ml) peanut oil

3   large parsnips, peeled and sliced into lengthwise strips with a vegetable peeler

2   ounces (55 g) Parmesan cheese

Salt

FOR THE GARNISHES:

Micro arugula

Fresh lemon juice

16   cornichons

a baking sheet as you make them. Place the patties in the refrigerator for 30 minutes (this will help them hold their shape).

Preheat the oven to 300°F (150°C).

Prep the foie gras: Place the foie gras in the freezer for 30 minutes (this makes it easier to slice). Remove the foie gras from the freezer and slice it into slider-size pieces (a little smaller than the buns). Place them in the refrigerator, then 10 minutes before cooking, move them back to the freezer.

Make the parsnip chips: While the patties are in the refrigerator, heat the oil in a deep-fryer or large saucepan to 350°F (175°C). Add the parsnip slices and fry until golden brown, about 5 minutes, working in batches so as not to crowd the fryer. Remove them to a wire rack or plate lined with paper towels. While they're still hot, grate the cheese over the parsnip chips with a Microplane, season with salt, and continue with the remaining parsnips.

Finish the sliders: Brush the cut sides of the pretzel buns with butter, place them in the oven, and toast them for about 4 minutes, until golden brown and slightly crisp.

Remove the patties from the refrigerator and season them with salt, pepper, garlic powder, and onion powder. Heat a large cast-iron skillet over high heat until almost smoking and add 1 tablespoon of the oil. Add five of the patties and cook for 2 minutes per side for medium rare. Remove the patties to a wire rack set over a baking sheet to rest. Finish cooking the patties in the same way in two more batches.

Cook the foie gras: Once all of the patties are cooked, remove the foie gras from the freezer and season it with salt and pepper. Heat a nonstick skillet over high heat until scorching hot. If you have an exhaust fan over your stove, now is the time to turn it on, as the foie gras will smoke a lot. Working in batches, add the foie gras and cook for about 30 seconds per side, until nicely browned. Move the slices to a wire rack set over a baking sheet and begin to assemble the sliders.

To assemble: Place large dollop of jam (about 1 tablespoon) on the bottom half of each bun; follow that with a beef patty and a piece of foie gras. Top it off with some micro arugula and a small squeeze of lemon. Set the top bun on top and run a skewer through a cornichon and through the middle of the slider to hold it all together. Place 3 sliders on each plate with the parsnip chips on the side and serve.

SALADS & SOUPS

My mother cooked with love for her family, and there is nothing
that tastes better. She comes from the era of a big bowl of salad
and bread with nearly every meal (it was almost always welcome,
though I will admit it was a little odd with fish sticks). Soup was
commonplace too, as it was quick to make; but I won't lie—that
world-famous tomato soup can was a go-to for my mom after
a rough day, and I still indulge in a bowlful once in a while. Salads
and soups have since changed drastically for me. I make a point
to elevate them above the expected, as they are easy to experiment with and simple to put together, the ingredients tend to
be fairly cheap, and the possibilities are endless.

In this chapter, you will find a variety of flavors from around
the world that come together in my personal take on the modern American table. Use the recipes as a starting point, and don't
be afraid to try new combinations such as different varieties of
mushrooms in the Pressure Cooked Cream of Mushroom Soup
(page 54), or throw a grilled chicken breast in with my Charred
Romaine salad (page 47) and call it a meal.

Spring Veggie Salad

with *Prosciutto and* Lemon Vinaigrette

Although there's no real springtime in Vegas, our neighbor California reliably supplies our farmers' markets with the bounty of the season. This spring salad is incredibly fresh and crisp, with the greens accented by my beloved prosciutto. Check out your local farmers' market for the salad greens—I promise you'll be able to tell the difference between freshly grown and shipped from who knows where. If your farmers' market doesn't have garlic chives, use regular chives or look for garlic chives in an Asian market.

▶ SERVES 4 TO 6 ◀

Make the lemon vinaigrette: In a medium bowl, combine the lemon juice, vinegar, mustard, and honey and whisk to dissolve the honey. Slowly add the oil, whisking constantly, until emulsified. Season with salt and pepper. You may have leftover dressing that you can use on another salad; it will keep refrigerated for up to 4 days.

Make the salad: In a large bowl, combine the asparagus, sliced sugar snap peas, arugula, garlic chives, pea shoots, parsley, and cilantro.

Bring a small pot of water to a boil and salt it. Add the reserved whole sugar snap peas and blanch them for just a few seconds, until just a little softened but still very crisp. Scoop the snap peas out with a slotted spoon and place them on a paper towel–lined plate to dry. Split them in half to expose the peas, trying to keep all the peas on one side.

To serve: Drizzle the vinaigrette over the salad and toss to lightly coat. Divide the salad among plates, top with the prosciutto and shaved Parmesan, and arrange the blanched peas around the salad.

FOR THE LEMON VINAIGRETTE:

- ¼ cup (60 ml) fresh lemon juice
- 1 tablespoon apple cider vinegar
- 1 teaspoon Dijon-style mustard
- 1 teaspoon honey
- ¼ cup (60 ml) extra-virgin olive oil
- Salt and freshly ground black pepper

FOR THE SPRING VEGGIE SALAD:

- 8 ounces (225 g) asparagus, stalks cut into ½-inch (12-mm) pieces
- 8 ounces (225 g) sugar snap peas, thinly sliced on a bias, plus 10 whole pods
- 1 cup (20 g) arugula leaves
- 20 garlic chives or regular chives, cut into ½-inch (12-mm) pieces
- 20 pea shoots
- ¼ cup (13 g) fresh parsley leaves, roughly chopped
- ¼ cup (10 g) fresh cilantro leaves, roughly chopped

FOR THE GARNISHES:

- 5 to 6 slices prosciutto, torn into bite-size pieces
- 2 ounces (55 g) shaved Parmesan cheese

Charred Romaine

with Pickled Watermelon, Candied Pecans, Blue Cheese, *and* Balsamic Vinaigrette

This salad has it all: sour from the pickled watermelon, sweet from the pecans, salty from the blue cheese, and bitter from the charred romaine. I like to char the romaine over an open flame for this recipe, so I usually make this salad when I've fired up the grill, but a cast-iron skillet or the broiler (place it flat-side up in a broiler pan) also will work. If you're using a skillet, char the romaine in batches so you don't crowd the pan. After you're done with the salad, you'll have extra candied pecans to snack on, if they last that long!

SERVES 4

Make the pickled watermelon: Cut the watermelon in half. Cut one half into ½-inch- (12-mm-) thick slices and remove the pink flesh of the watermelon from the rind. Discard the watermelon rind. Cut the watermelon flesh into roughly ½-inch (12-mm) cubes, put them into a large Mason jar, and put them in the refrigerator.

Remove the pink flesh from the rind of the remaining half of the watermelon and chop it. Discard the rind, place the watermelon flesh in a blender, and blend on high speed for about 3 minutes, until liquefied. Line a fine-mesh strainer with a double piece of cheesecloth and strain the watermelon juice into a medium bowl. Measure out 1 cup (240 ml) of the juice; if there's any extra, you can drink it.

Toast the pickling spice in a small sauté pan over medium heat, stirring often, for 5 minutes, or until fragrant. Pour in the white wine vinegar, apple cider vinegar, sugar, and salt; bring them to a boil and cook for about 5 minutes, until reduced by half. Remove

(recipe continues)

FOR THE PICKLED WATERMELON:

1 small (about 4 pounds/1.8 kg) seedless watermelon
2 tablespoons pickling spice
½ cup (120 ml) white wine vinegar
½ cup (120 ml) apple cider vinegar
¼ cup (50 g) granulated sugar
3 tablespoons salt

FOR THE CANDIED PECANS:

1½ cups (150 g) pecan halves
2 large egg whites
¼ cup (55 g) packed brown sugar
1 teaspoon ground cayenne
1 teaspoon salt

FOR THE BALSAMIC VINAIGRETTE:

¼ cup (60 ml) balsamic vinegar
1 tablespoon fresh lemon juice
1 teaspoon Dijon-style mustard
½ cup (120 ml) extra-virgin olive oil
Salt and freshly ground black pepper

FOR THE SALAD:

4 hearts of romaine, cut in half lengthwise
2 tablespoons extra-virgin olive oil
Salt and freshly ground black pepper
1 cup (135 g) crumbled blue cheese

the pan from the heat and pour in the water-melon juice. Set it aside to cool for 10 minutes, then pour the mixture through a fine-mesh strainer into a small bowl.

Remove the chopped watermelon from the refrigerator and pour the watermelon juice mixture over the watermelon. Cover and return to the refrigerator to pickle for 1 hour. After plating, any remaining watermelon can be kept in the brine and enjoyed for up to 4 days (the liquid may become a little cloudy, but don't worry; it's completely normal).

Make the candied pecans: Preheat the oven to 300°F (150°C) and line a baking sheet with a silicone mat.

Place the pecans in a medium bowl. In a separate bowl, whisk the egg whites until they begin to get frothy and turn white. Pour the egg whites over the pecans and stir well with a wooden spoon to coat all of the nuts. Combine the brown sugar, cayenne, and salt in a small bowl and whisk to break up any clumps of brown sugar. Add the brown sugar mixture to the pecans and stir to evenly coat the pecans. Spread the pecans over the prepared

baking sheet in a single layer and toast for about 20 minutes, stirring with a heatproof spatula about halfway through, until they are completely dry and deep brown in color. Set them aside to cool.

Make the balsamic vinaigrette: In a small bowl, whisk together the vinegar, lemon juice, and mustard. Slowly drizzle in the oil, whisking constantly until emulsified. Season with salt and pepper.

Make the salad: Brush the cut side of each romaine half with oil and season liberally with salt and pepper. Place the romaine hearts cut-side down on an extremely hot grill (I prefer a charcoal grill; see the headnote for indoor alternatives). Grill for 2 minutes, or until some of the lettuce takes on a nice black char. Watch it carefully so it does not burn.

To plate: Place the romaine wedges on plates and sprinkle the pickled watermelon, candied pecans, and crumbled blue cheese on and around the wedges. Drizzle on the vinaigrette and finish with some pepper.

King Crab and Compressed Watermelon Salad

A great summer salad is light and refreshing, and this salad is just that. King crab pairs perfectly with sweet summer watermelon. The briny crab is offset by the subtle flavor of watermelon, and a simple lemon vinaigrette pulls the two together. The original recipe calls for a vacuum sealer, but as they aren't commonly found in home kitchens, I designed this version to be made with or without one. Unless you are extremely lucky, your fishmonger will only have frozen crab, but if you find fresh, definitely grab it! After you poach the crab, you'll have a lot of delicious crab-infused butter left—strain it and spread it over toast or use it in place of plain butter in another recipe.

➡ SERVES 4 ⬅

Make the lemon vinaigrette: In a small bowl, whisk together the lemon zest, lemon juice, honey, and mustard. Slowly add the oil, whisking constantly until emulsified. Season with salt and pepper.

Make the compressed watermelon: Slice the watermelon into ¼-inch (6-mm) rounds. From the middle of each watermelon round, cut out a 2½ by 1-inch (6 by 2.5-cm) rectangle. Select the four best rectangles (use the remaining watermelon for my Charred Romaine recipe on page 47 or enjoy it as a snack). Place the watermelon in a vacuum seal bag, if using. Pour in the lemon vinaigrette and gently mix the vinaigrette around the bag. Position the watermelon pieces in a flat layer, seal the bag with a vacuum sealer, and place in the refrigerator for 30 minutes.

(recipe continues)

FOR THE LEMON VINAIGRETTE:

Grated zest of ½ lemon

¼ cup (60 ml) fresh lemon juice

1 tablespoon honey

½ cup (120 ml) extra-virgin olive oil

Salt and freshly ground black pepper

FOR THE COMPRESSED WATERMELON:

1 very small (about 3 pounds) seedless watermelon

FOR THE BUTTER-POACHED KING CRAB:

4 large king crab legs (no claws)

3 sticks (12 ounces/340 g) unsalted butter

¼ cup (60 ml) fresh lemon juice

FOR THE GARNISHES:

Radish microgreens

Micro arugula

Maldon sea salt

If you're not using a vacuum sealer, place the watermelon in a large zip-top bag. Pour in the lemon vinaigrette and gently mix the vinaigrette around the bag. Position the watermelon pieces in a flat layer and seal the bag, removing as much air as possible. Place the bag on a large flat plate and place another plate on top of it. Place a weight on top, such as a couple of canned goods or bags of beans, to compress the watermelon. Place in the refrigerator for 2 hours. The watermelon won't compress as much as if you used the vacuum sealer, but it will still taste great, and that's the most important thing! Remove the watermelon from the dressing and reserve the dressing for the end.

Make the butter-poached king crab: Defrost the crab legs if necessary. To remove the meat from the crab, cut the legs in half at the joint. Use kitchen shears to cut through the length of the shell and remove the meat, with a goal of removing the largest section of the leg in one whole piece. Set the long pieces aside and break down the rest of the meat by tearing it with your fingers.

In a medium saucepan, melt the butter over medium heat and add 2 tablespoons water and the lemon juice. Add the shredded crab meat and cook for 3 minutes, then remove the meat with a slotted spoon and place it in a mesh strainer so the excess butter can drip off. Place the large leg pieces in the butter and simmer for 3 minutes to cook through. Remove the leg pieces from the butter, set them on a plate, and pat off the excess butter with a paper towel.

To serve: Place a piece of compressed watermelon a little off the center of each plate and top with some shredded crab, followed by a whole leg piece. Garnish the top of the legs with radish microgreens, micro arugula, and a small sprinkle of salt. Finish by drizzling the reserved lemon vinaigrette over the top.

Asian Steak Salad

I am lucky to live in a city that has a decent Chinatown, and I go there often. The markets there are always filled with life—from the fish swimming around in tanks, to the hordes of people placing their orders, it's sensory overload at all times. While there are a lot of ingredients in this salad, almost all of them are staple pantry ingredients that you can get at your local Asian food store and many supermarkets. The method is very simple, with a decidedly delicious outcome. The dressing will make more than you need here; it keeps for up to 4 days in the refrigerator and goes great with any salad, or use it as a marinade for chicken or a firm-fleshed fish.

➤ SERVES 4 TO 6 ◀

Marinate the steak: In a medium bowl, combine the ginger, garlic, cilantro, soy sauce, lime zest, lime juice, fish sauce, ponzu sauce, hoisin sauce, sambal oelek, 2 tablespoons of the olive oil, the sesame oil, and brown sugar and whisk to dissolve the sugar. Season with salt and pepper. Place the steaks in a zip-top bag, pour the marinade over the top, and seal the bag. Massage the marinade into the steaks for 2 minutes, then refrigerate to marinate for at least 1 hour or up to overnight.

Make the dressing: In a medium bowl, combine the lime zest, lime juice, sambal oelek, fish sauce, honey, roasted garlic, rice vinegar, soy sauce, ponzu sauce, and sesame oil and whisk well to break down the roasted garlic cloves and emulsify the dressing. Set aside until ready to serve.

Cook the steaks: Remove the steaks from the marinade and place them on a wire rack set over a baking sheet. Using paper towels, wipe away as much of the marinade as possible (so you can get a good sear on them).

(recipe continues)

FOR THE ASIAN STEAK AND MARINADE:

1 ½-inch (12-mm) piece fresh ginger, grated

2 cloves garlic, smashed and diced

1 tablespoon chopped fresh cilantro

¼ cup (60 ml) soy sauce

Zest of ½ lime

2 tablespoons fresh lime juice

1½ teaspoons fish sauce

1½ teaspoons ponzu sauce

1½ teaspoons hoisin sauce

1 tablespoon sambal oelek (chili-garlic paste)

3 tablespoons extra-virgin olive oil

1 tablespoon toasted sesame oil

2 tablespoons brown sugar

Salt and freshly ground black pepper

1 pound (455 g) skirt steak

FOR THE DRESSING:

1 tablespoon grated lime zest

¼ cup (60 ml) fresh lime juice

¼ cup (60 ml) sambal oelek (chili-garlic paste)

1 tablespoon fish sauce

2 tablespoons honey

3 cloves Roasted Garlic (page 16)

1 tablespoon rice vinegar

2 tablespoons soy sauce

2 tablespoons ponzu sauce

2 tablespoons toasted sesame oil

(ingredients continue)

Allow the steaks to come to room temperature, 15 to 20 minutes.

Place a large cast-iron skillet over high heat until it's almost smoking. Add the remaining 1 tablespoon olive oil and swirl it around the pan. Season one of the steaks lightly with salt and pepper on both sides. Add the steak to the pan and cook for about 3 minutes on each side for medium rare. Remove the steak to a clean wire rack placed over a baking sheet. Let the steaks rest for 10 minutes, then cut them into ½-inch- (12-mm-) thick (or thinner if you prefer) slices against the grain.

Make the salad: Cook the noodles according to package directions; drain and let them cool.

In a large bowl, combine the noodles, arugula, watercress, bell pepper, scallions, cilantro, mint, peanuts, and radishes and toss well. Drizzle the dressing over the salad 1 tablespoon at a time, tossing constantly until the salad is lightly coated.

To plate: Divide the steak among the plates, top with about 1 cup (75 g) of the salad, and finish with the radish sprouts and radish microgreens.

FOR THE SALAD:

4 ounces (115 g) lo mein noodles

4 cups (80 g) arugula

2 cups (70 g) watercress

1 red bell pepper, julienned

3 scallions, thinly sliced on a bias

¼ cup (10 g) finely chopped fresh cilantro

¼ cup (13 g) finely chopped fresh mint

¼ cup (40 g) peanuts, toasted and lightly crushed

4 radishes, very thinly sliced

FOR THE GARNISHES:

Radish sprouts

Radish microgreens

Pressure Cooked Cream of Mushroom Soup

I am a big fan of mushrooms in all shapes and sizes, so for this recipe I use four different varieties to give the soup some serious depth of flavor. If you can't find these specific mushrooms, use what you can find, but try to include at least three different varieties to get the complexity that makes this soup stand out. The best way to arrive at this soup's silky smooth texture is by making it in a pressure cooker. If you don't own a pressure cooker, you can cook the soup in a large pot on the stove-top (simmer covered for 1 hour); the outcome will be slightly less silky, but still absolutely delicious. Save the best-looking porcinis for garnish and cook the rest in the soup. Serve this super-rich soup in small portions.

▶ SERVES 4 ◀

Make the mushroom soup: Tie the bay leaves, parsley, thyme, and rosemary with butcher's twine to make a bouquet garni and set aside. Heat the oil in a pressure cooker over medium heat. Add the shallot and cook for 5 minutes, or until translucent. Add the roasted garlic and mushrooms and cook, stirring often, until the mushrooms are softened, about 10 minutes. Add the vinegar and cook, stirring, until it is almost all absorbed. Add the wine and cook for about 5 minutes, stirring often, until it is almost all absorbed. Add the stock, season with salt and pepper, and bring to a simmer. Add the bouquet garni. Close the pressure cooker and cook at high pressure for 20 minutes. Turn off the heat, carefully release the steam, and wait until the pressure is fully released to open the pressure cooker.

FOR THE MUSHROOM SOUP:

2   bay leaves

4   sprigs fresh flat-leaf parsley

2   sprigs fresh thyme

1   sprig fresh rosemary

2   tablespoons extra-virgin olive oil

1   large shallot, roughly chopped

4   cloves Roasted Garlic (page 16)

6   ounces (170 g) fresh shiitake mushrooms, stemmed and roughly chopped

8   ounces (225 g) fresh baby bella mushrooms, roughly chopped

6   ounces (170 g) fresh button mushrooms, roughly chopped

3   fresh porcini mushrooms, roughly chopped

¼   cup (60 ml) sherry vinegar

¼   cup (60 ml) dry white wine, such as Pinot Grigio

2½ cups (600 ml) Chicken Stock (page 20), plus more if needed

Salt and freshly ground black pepper

1   cup (240 ml) heavy cream

FOR THE GARNISHES:

2   tablespoons extra-virgin olive oil

2   fresh porcini mushrooms, sliced lengthwise ⅛ inch (3 mm) thick

Salt and freshly ground black pepper

12 fresh flat-leaf parsley leaves

Maldon sea salt

Truffle oil

Remove the herb bundle and any herb stems that might have come loose. Transfer the mushroom mixture to a blender and blend on high speed until very smooth, 2 to 3 minutes. Pour the soup into a medium saucepan and stir in the cream. Bring to a simmer over medium heat, then reduce the heat to medium-low and cook, stirring very often, for 8 minutes, or until just bubbling. Season with salt and pepper.

Make the porcini mushroom garnish: Heat the oil in a small cast-iron skillet over high heat. Add the porcini mushrooms and sear for about 2 minutes on each side, until nicely browned. Season with salt and pepper.

To serve: Divide the soup among serving bowls, top with the seared porcini slices, and scatter the parsley leaves on top. Sprinkle with a little Maldon salt and a small drizzle of truffle oil and serve.

Lobster Bisque

with Cognac Crema and Bacon Fat Croutons

Lobster bisque was one of my father's favorite foods, although I never had a chance to make it for him. Toward the end of his life, his best friend opened up an amazing little restaurant in Waterloo, Iowa, near where my dad lived, and this place had a lobster bisque that my dad loved. Unfortunately, my dad's friend no longer owns the restaurant, so I had to develop my own lobster bisque recipe to get my fix.

You'll be poaching the lobster tails in butter and making a flavored butter with the shells. I like to reserve the claws and little legs for my Lobster Ravioli (page 66) to get two amazing dinners out of one high-ticket item. If you're not planning to make the ravioli, you can poach the claws with the tails and throw the legs in with the shells for making the bisque. After you poach the tails, you'll have a lot of delicious lobster-infused butter left; strain it and spread it over toast or use it in place of plain butter in another recipe. To light the cognac, you will need a stick lighter—a long lighter used to light a charcoal grill. This is the safest way to ignite the alcohol, so please invest the three dollars in a stick lighter before making this recipe.

➤ SERVES 4 ◄

Prepare the lobsters: Fill a bowl large enough to fit the lobsters with ice and water to make an ice water bath. Bring a large pot of water to a rapid boil and salt it. Dispatch the lobsters by driving a knife straight down through the top of the head, then pull the knife forward like you are squeezing a lemon with a citrus squeezer. Immediately place the lobsters in the boiling water and poach for 2 minutes (if your pot isn't big enough to hold all three lobsters, poach them one at a time). After each

(recipe continues)

FOR THE LOBSTER BISQUE:

Salt

3   (1½-pound/680-g) live lobsters

12 sprigs fresh flat-leaf parsley

6   sprigs fresh thyme

2   bay leaves

2   tablespoons extra-virgin olive oil

1   stick (4 ounces/115 g) unsalted butter

½   cup (120 ml) cognac

1   yellow onion, finely diced

2   shallots, minced

2   stalks celery, minced

2   carrots, finely diced

4   cloves garlic, smashed

3   tablespoons tomato paste

2   tablespoons sherry vinegar

1   cup (240 ml) dry white wine, such as Pinot Grigio

5   cups (1.2 L) Shellfish Stock (page 21)

1   cup (240 ml) heavy cream

Pinch of ground cayenne

Freshly ground black pepper

5   large egg yolks

2   tablespoons cornstarch

Chopped fresh chives

FOR THE BACON FAT CROUTONS:

½   French baguette

5   strips bacon

1   tablespoon olive oil

1   teaspoon dried thyme

Salt and freshly ground black pepper

(ingredients continue)

lobster is poached, move it to the ice water bath to stop the cooking and let it cool completely. Break down each lobster by twisting off the tail, claws, and all the little legs. Either save the claws and legs to use in my Lobster Ravioli (page 66) or remove the meat and save it to poach later. Separate the body and clean out the intestinal tract. Reserve all of the shells. Cut the tail meat out of the shell with kitchen shears and set the meat aside to use later; reserve the shells from the tails as well.

Wrap the parsley, thyme, and bay leaves in a piece of cheesecloth, then tie it with kitchen twine to make a bouquet garni; set aside.

Using your hands or a knife, break the shells down into pieces that easily fit in a pan. In a large saucepan, heat the oil over medium-high heat. Add the lobster shells and cook until the shells turn bright red, about 7 minutes. Add the butter and cook for 5 minutes, then strain the butter into a large, heavy-bottomed skillet and reserve it, returning the shells to the first pan. Reduce the heat under the pan with the shells to medium. Pour the cognac over the shells and, using a stick lighter, light the cognac and cook until the flames stop. Turn off the heat and set aside.

Heat the butter in the skillet over medium-high heat. Add the onion, shallots, celery, carrots, and garlic and cook for 10 minutes, or until the vegetables begin to soften. Add the tomato paste and cook for another 5 minutes. Deglaze the pan with the vinegar and cook for 2 minutes. Transfer the vegetables to the pot with the shells and place it over medium-high heat. Add the wine and reduce by half, about 8 minutes. Pour in the shellfish stock and cream, add the bouquet garni, and season with cayenne, salt, and pepper. Bring it to a simmer, then reduce the heat to medium-low, partially cover, and simmer for 1 hour.

Make the bacon croutons: Preheat the oven to 300°F (150°C).

Cut the baguette into crouton-size pieces. In a large skillet over medium-high heat, cook the bacon until the fat is rendered and the bacon is crisp (we are only using the fat here, so enjoy the bacon as a cook's snack). Add the oil to the pan, then add the croutons and cook for 5 minutes, stirring frequently to coat all the croutons

FOR THE COGNAC CREMA:

½ cup (120 ml) cognac

½ cup (120 ml) Mexican crema

Salt and freshly ground black pepper

FOR THE BUTTER-POACHED LOBSTER TAILS:

3 sticks (12 ounces/340 g) unsalted butter

Zest and juice of 1 lemon

Salt

with the bacon fat and lightly color them. Crumble in the thyme and season with salt and pepper. Remove the croutons to a baking sheet, place them in the oven, and bake until crisp, about 10 minutes. Remove and set aside for plating.

Make the cognac crema: In a small saucepan, bring the cognac to a boil over medium-high heat and boil until reduced by half, about 7 minutes. Remove from the heat and set aside to cool. Stir in the crema, season with salt and pepper, and stir well to combine. Transfer the cognac crema to a squeeze bottle and set aside for plating.

Finish the lobster bisque: Strain the bisque through a fine-mesh strainer into a bowl and clean your pot of any small solids that may have been left behind. Return the bisque to the pot and place it over medium heat.

In a medium bowl, whisk the egg yolks with the cornstarch until smooth. Take ¼ cup (60 ml) of the bisque and slowly whisk it into the egg yolk mixture to temper the eggs. Whisk the tempered egg yolk mixture into the pot of bisque and continue to cook, stirring frequently, for about 15 minutes, until the bisque has thickened up and is silky smooth.

Make the butter-poached lobster tails: While the bisque is simmering, in a small saucepan, melt the butter over medium heat and add the lemon zest and juice. Place the lobster tails (and claws and legs if you aren't saving them for the lobster ravioli) in the butter, reduce the heat to medium-low, and poach them for about 5 minutes, until the lobster is just heated through. Remove the meat to a plate and lightly pat the tails with a paper towel to remove excess butter, then slice them ½ inch (12 mm) thick. Season with salt.

To serve: Divide the bisque among serving bowls and arrange the lobster tail pieces over the top. Add a few bacon croutons and gently squeeze some crema over the bisque, getting creative with your design to personalize your bowls. Top the bowls off with some chives and a drizzle of extra-virgin olive oil and serve.

PASTA & RISOTTO

There is something therapeutic about making pasta by hand.
It's relaxing and stressful, calming and aggravating all at the same
time. It's a rewarding feeling when you see a perfect sheet of
pasta coming through the pasta roller, but a heartbreaking night-
mare when it is done wrong. Perfecting handmade pasta takes
years, and I by no means deem myself an expert. With food, you
can never stop learning. Chef Ramsay told us that in his younger
years, long before the Michelin stars, his mentor would have
him make endless amounts of pasta while blindfolded. That is
extreme dedication!

In Italy, pasta is taken more seriously than politics and every
region swears their way is the best way. People dedicate their
lives to making one type of pasta all day every day for decades.
It is inspiring to see and even more inspiring to eat! There are
hundreds, if not thousands, of ways to make pasta, and it comes
in every shape imaginable. I have even found *sombreroni* pasta,
shaped like a Mexican sombrero!

I usually make my pasta the old-fashioned way, with a pile
of flour and eggs on my cutting board, but for the purposes
of this book, I use a food processor to ensure a consistent outcome for even the most novice pasta maker. This chapter brings
traditional pasta to the modern table with recipes such as my
Bourbon-Braised Short Rib Ravioli (page 69) and Sweetbread
Tortellini (page 72)—neither short ribs nor sweetbreads are
commonly used as fillings, but when handled with care, they
make for a perfect plate of pasta.

Homemade Fettuccine

with All-Day Red Sauce *and* Garlic Bread

I ate a lot of pasta when I was a kid, but in the eighties and nineties, pasta and red sauce most often would come from a box and a can. My home was no exception, although my mom cooked with love and always added her own touches to the sauce. Mom would whip up some great garlic bread, too, and that's what made pasta nights really memorable for me. Now red sauce is something I make all the time, and I have honed it in to what I consider a damn near perfect recipe. Don't be turned off by the anchovies—they add a deep saltiness to the sauce without even a hint of fish flavor. The red sauce makes more than you'll need for the fettuccine—about 1 quart (960 ml)—so you'll have plenty left to make my Lazy Day Chicken Parmesan (page 110).

➤ SERVES 4 ◄

Make the red sauce: Wrap the basil, rosemary, thyme, and bay leaves in cheesecloth and tie with butcher's twine to make a bouquet garni. Set aside. Heat the oil in a large saucepan over medium heat. Add the onions, celery, carrots, and fresh garlic and season with salt and pepper. Cook, stirring occasionally, for 10 to 15 minutes, until the vegetables start to soften. Squeeze in the roasted garlic, add the anchovies, and continue to cook for about 10 minutes, stirring occasionally, until the vegetables are translucent and the anchovies have melted away. Add the tomato paste and cook, stirring often, until the sauce emits a roasted tomato scent, about 5 minutes, keeping a close watch so the paste doesn't burn. Pour in the wine and vinegar and stir to release

(recipe continues)

FOR THE ALL-DAY RED SAUCE:

8 fresh basil leaves

Leaves from 1 sprig fresh rosemary

Leaves from 2 sprigs fresh thyme

2 bay leaves

3 tablespoons extra-virgin olive oil

3 medium yellow onions, finely diced

2 stalks celery, finely diced

2 carrots, finely diced

5 cloves fresh garlic, finely minced or pressed through a garlic press

Salt and freshly ground black pepper

½ head Roasted Garlic (page 16)

3 canned anchovies in oil

¼ cup (60 ml) tomato paste

1 cup (240 ml) red wine, such as Cabernet or Merlot

¼ cup (60 ml) balsamic vinegar

2 cups (480 ml) Chicken Stock (page 20) or Vegetable Stock (page 19), plus more if needed

2 (28-ounce/785-g) cans whole San Marzano tomatoes, with juices

FOR THE FETTUCCINE:

2 cups (250 g) all-purpose flour, plus more for dusting

2 large eggs

4 large egg yolks

1 teaspoon salt

Semolina flour for dusting

½ cup (50 g) finely grated Parmesan cheese

(ingredients continue)

any browned bits from the bottom of the pan. Increase the heat to medium-high and cook until the liquid is reduced by half, about 5 minutes. Add the bouquet garni to the sauce and season with salt and pepper. Pour in the stock, bring it to a simmer, then reduce the heat to medium and cook for 15 minutes to infuse the stock with the flavor of the herbs. Add the tomatoes, crushing them in with your hands. Bring them to a simmer, then reduce the heat to low and cook, stirring occasionally, for at least 2 hours and up to 5 hours, adding a little stock if the sauce gets too thick. The longer the sauce cooks, the more concentrated the flavors will become.

Remove the bouquet garni from the sauce, taste, and season it with salt and pepper if needed. Puree the sauce with an immersion blender or in batches in a blender until smooth. The sauce will keep in a covered container in the refrigerator for up to 4 days and in the freezer for up to 1 month.

Make the fettuccine: Combine the all-purpose flour, whole eggs, egg yolks, and salt in the bowl of a food processor fitted with the blade and pulse until combined. Add 1 tablespoon cold water and pulse until the mixture looks like wet sand and holds its shape when formed into a small ball. If the dough seems too sticky, add a bit more flour. If the dough is too dry, add another teaspoon of water, pulse again, and check. Continue adding 1 teaspoon of water at a time until you reach the correct consistency. Move the dough to a floured surface and knead until the dough is smooth, solid, and elastic, 2 to 3 minutes. Tightly wrap the dough in plastic wrap and leave it on the counter to rest for 1 hour, or refrigerate it for up to 1 day (take it out of the refrigerator to rest, covered, at room temperature for 1 hour before you roll it out).

Line a baking sheet with parchment paper and sprinkle it generously with semolina flour. Lightly dust the work surface with semolina flour. Cut off one quarter of the dough and wrap the remaining dough in plastic wrap. Dust the dough lightly with flour and flatten it out with your hands into a rectangle. Roll the pasta through

FOR THE GARLIC BREAD:

- 1 sourdough baguette (about 14 ounces/400 g)
- ½ head Roasted Garlic (page 16)
- ½ cup (115 g) Roasted Garlic–Rosemary Butter (page 18), at room temperature

FOR THE GARNISHES:

Parmesan cheese, finely grated on a Microplane

Small fresh basil leaves

the thickest setting of your pasta machine twice, continuing to flour the dough to prevent sticking, as needed. Set the machine to the next lowest setting and repeat the rolling process all the way through to the third smallest setting (I like my fettuccine to be a little thicker, so I stop there, but feel free to go one setting lower, though I don't recommend using the smallest setting because it may make your fettuccine too fragile to work with). Slice the pasta sheet in half and run the sheet through the pasta machine's fettuccine cutter. As the fettuccine comes out of the machine, lightly grasp the strands and form them into a small nest, dusting it with semolina flour as you set it down on the baking sheet. Repeat with the remaining dough to complete eight fettuccine nests.

Make the garlic bread: Preheat the oven to 350°F (175°C).

Cut the baguette in half lengthwise. In a small bowl, squeeze the roasted garlic into the roasted garlic–rosemary butter and, using a fork, mash the ingredients together. Spread the butter over the cut sides of the baguette halves and place them onto a baking sheet. Bake for 15 to 20 minutes, until the edges are golden brown and crunchy.

Cook the fettuccine: Place a large pot of salted water over high heat and bring it to a rapid boil. Add four fettuccine nests to the water and cook for 2 minutes, or until they are al dente. While the pasta cooks, add 1½ cups (360 ml) of the red sauce to a large skillet over medium heat. Transfer the cooked pasta to the pan and add about 2 tablespoons of the pasta water, then toss to finish cooking the pasta and coat it with the sauce. Toss with ¼ cup (25 g) of the cheese and season with salt and pepper. Repeat to cook the remaining four pasta nests.

To serve: Spin one quarter of the fettuccine around a pair of tongs until you have a nice solid ball of pasta. Place it in the middle of a large plate or bowl and top it with a huge helping of cheese. Finish with a few small basil leaves and serve with the garlic bread on the side. Repeat to make four servings.

Lobster Ravioli
with Lemon Cream Sauce

Did you know that lobster was considered trash food and was served to prisoners and the very poor in the 1800s and early 1900s? We've come a long way with lobster! I created this recipe to make use of the leftover claws and legs from my Lobster Bisque (page 56). Those little pockets of lobster meat are incredibly tender, and mixed with the meat from the claw they make a perfect ravioli filling. You will need a small wooden dowel, easily found at your local hardware store, to get the meat out of the little legs. If you haven't made the bisque, simply go for the 8 ounces (225 g) prepared lobster meat called for in the ingredients list. If you happen to have extra lobster claws, follow the directions for the butter-poached lobster tails with my Lobster Bisque recipe and serve the claw meat on top.

➤ SERVES 4 ◀

Make the lobster filling: Place the lobster meat in a medium bowl. Add the mascarpone, egg, flour, and tarragon and mix lightly to combine, taking care not to break the lobster meat apart. Season with salt and pepper. Cover the bowl with plastic wrap and place the filling in the refrigerator until you are ready to stuff the ravioli.

Make the pasta dough: In the bowl of a food processor fitted with the blade, combine the all-purpose flour, whole eggs, egg yolks, and salt and pulse until combined. Add 1 tablespoon cold water and pulse until the mixture looks like wet sand and holds its shape when formed into a small ball. If the dough seems too sticky, add a bit more flour. If the dough is too dry, add another teaspoon of water, pulse again, and check. Continue adding 1 teaspoon of water at a time until you reach the correct consistency. Move the dough to a floured surface and knead until it is smooth, solid, and elastic,

FOR THE LOBSTER RAVIOLI FILLING:

- 8 ounces (225 g) lobster meat
- ½ cup plus 2 tablespoons (150 ml) mascarpone cheese
- 1 large egg, lightly beaten
- 1 tablespoon all-purpose flour
- 1 tablespoon minced fresh tarragon

Salt and freshly ground black pepper

FOR THE PASTA DOUGH:

- 2 cups (250 g) all-purpose flour, plus more for dusting
- 2 large eggs
- 4 large egg yolks
- 1 teaspoon salt

Semolina flour for dusting

FOR THE SHELLFISH REDUCTION:

- 1 tablespoon extra-virgin olive oil
- 1 carrot, finely diced
- 2 stalks celery, finely diced
- 1 large shallot, minced
- 3 cloves garlic, minced
- ½ cup (120 ml) Pernod
- 1½ cups (360 ml) Shellfish Stock (page 21)
- ½ stick (2 ounces/55 g) unsalted butter

Salt and freshly ground black pepper

2 to 3 minutes. Tightly wrap the dough in plastic wrap and leave it on the counter to rest for 1 hour, or refrigerate it for up to 1 day (take it out of the refrigerator to rest, covered, at room temperature for 1 hour before you roll it out).

Line a baking sheet with parchment paper and sprinkle it generously with semolina flour. Lightly dust the work surface with semolina flour. Cut off one quarter of the dough and wrap the remaining dough in plastic wrap. Dust the dough lightly with flour and flatten it out with your hands into a rectangle. Roll the pasta through the thickest setting of your pasta machine twice, continuing to flour the dough to prevent sticking, as needed. Set the machine to the next lowest setting and repeat the rolling process all the way through to the second to lowest setting. You should be able to see through the pasta sheet, but it should not tear. If the pasta becomes too long to handle, cut it in half. Once the pasta sheet is rolled out, dust it lightly with semolina flour, set it onto the prepared baking sheet, and cover with a slightly dampened clean kitchen towel. Repeat with the remaining dough, laying a sheet of plastic wrap between each finished pasta sheet before adding the next, ending with a damp towel on top.

Fill the ravioli: Line a baking sheet with parchment paper and dust it with semolina flour. Lay one pasta sheet onto your work surface and make two rows down the pasta sheet of 1-tablespoon portions of filling, setting them diagonally in a zigzag-like pattern and leaving 1 inch (2.5 cm) of space around each mound of filling. Dip your finger in a small bowl of water and run your finger around the edges of the filling to help the pasta stick together. Place a second sheet of pasta on top of the filling, very gently stretching the dough to reach and meet the edges of the bottom pasta sheet. Carefully work your way down the sheet and around each ravioli, sealing in the filling as you go. It is important to get out all of the air in the filling pocket so the ravioli don't explode when cooking. Using a 3-inch (7.5-cm) round cutter, cut the ravioli and place them onto the baking sheet. Cover with plastic wrap and place them in the refrigerator until ready to cook.

(recipe continues)

FOR THE LEMON CREAM SAUCE:

1   tablespoon extra-virgin olive oil

1   large shallot, minced

3   cloves garlic, minced

1½ cups (360 ml) dry white wine, such as Pinot Grigio

1   cup (240 ml) heavy cream

Zest of 2 lemons

2   tablespoons unsalted butter

Salt and freshly ground white pepper

FOR THE GARNISHES:

Small fresh flat-leaf parsley leaves

Minced fresh chives

Shaved Parmesan cheese

Finely grated lemon zest

Make the shellfish reduction: Heat the oil in a large skillet over medium heat. Add the carrots and celery and cook for 2 minutes, or until they begin to soften. Add the shallot and garlic and cook, stirring frequently, for 2 minutes, or until the vegetables are translucent and lightly colored. Pour in the Pernod and carefully ignite it with a stick lighter. When the flame has died out, add the stock, increase the heat to medium-high, and bring it to a boil. Cook until the liquid is reduced by half, about 8 minutes. Strain the reduction through a fine-mesh strainer, wipe out the skillet of any solids, and return the reduction to the pan. Place it over medium-high heat, bring to a boil, and cook for 3 minutes, or until the liquid lightly coats the back of a spoon. Turn off the heat and whisk in the butter 1 tablespoon at a time. Season with salt and pepper. Transfer the sauce to a squeeze bottle and set it aside for plating.

Make the cream sauce: In a large skillet, heat the oil over medium heat. Add the shallot and cook until translucent, about 2 minutes. Add the garlic and continue to cook for another 2 minutes, or until softened. Pour in the wine, increase the heat to high, and bring it to a boil. Reduce the heat to medium-high and cook for 10 minutes, or until the liquid is reduced to ¼ cup (60 ml). Pour in the cream and continue cooking for about 4 minutes, until the cream thickens slightly. Strain the sauce through a fine-mesh strainer, wipe the skillet clean of any solids, and return the sauce to the skillet. Turn the heat to medium-high, add the lemon zest, and cook, whisking continuously, for 3 minutes, or until the sauce thickly coats the back of a spoon. Turn off the heat and whisk in the butter 1 tablespoon at a time to thicken the sauce. Season with salt and pepper.

Cook the ravioli: Place a large pot of salted water over high heat and bring it to a rolling boil. Add 10 ravioli and cook for 2 minutes, or until the ravioli begin to float. While the ravioli are cooking, reheat the cream sauce over low heat until simmering. Add the ravioli to the skillet along with 2 teaspoons of the pasta cooking liquid and cook, basting for 1 minute to lightly coat the pasta, then use a slotted spoon to remove them to plates. Spoon a little of the sauce over the ravioli. Repeat with the remaining ravioli.

To serve: Place 5 ravioli on each plate and squeeze the lobster reduction in a circle around the plate over the ravioli. Garnish with some parsley, chives, shaved Parmesan, and lemon zest and serve.

Bourbon-Braised Short Rib Ravioli

This is a modern American spin on a traditional beef ravioli, with the filling made with my **Bourbon-Braised Short Ribs (page 128)**. So if you're making the ribs, save half of the meat to put into the ravioli. This recipe may not be for beginners, as it is fairly time-consuming to make, but you'll find it is more than worth your effort.

▶ SERVES 4 ◀

Make the ravioli filling: In a large bowl, combine the short rib meat, bell pepper, flour, ricotta, and egg and mix well to combine. Season with salt and pepper. Transfer the mixture to a food processor fitted with the blade attachment and pulse for about 20 seconds to blend the filling. Scoop the filling into generous 1-tablespoon mounds and set them onto a large plate. Cover with plastic wrap and refrigerate until you are ready to assemble the ravioli.

Make the ravioli: Line a baking sheet with parchment paper and sprinkle it generously with semolina flour. Lightly dust the work surface with semolina flour. Cut off one quarter of the pasta dough and wrap the remaining dough in plastic wrap. Dust the dough lightly with flour and flatten it out with your hands into a rectangle. Roll the pasta through the thickest setting of your pasta machine twice, continuing to flour the dough to prevent sticking, as needed. Set the machine to the next lowest setting and repeat the rolling process until you reach the next to lowest setting. You should be able to see through the pasta sheet, but it should not tear. If the pasta becomes too long to handle, cut it in half. Once the pasta sheet is rolled out, dust it lightly with semolina flour, set it onto the prepared baking sheet, and cover

(recipe continues)

FOR THE RAVIOLI FILLING:

½   batch Bourbon-Braised Short Ribs (page 128), shredded to equal 3 cups

1   small roasted red bell pepper (see page 18), diced

1   tablespoon all-purpose flour

½   cup (120 ml) ricotta cheese

1   whole egg, lightly beaten

Salt and freshly ground black pepper

PASTA DOUGH (SEE PAGE 66)

FOR THE HORSERADISH CREAM:

¼   cup (60 ml) crème fraîche

¼   cup (60 ml) prepared horseradish

1   tablespoon fresh lemon juice

Salt and freshly ground white pepper

FOR THE BOURBON BRAISING SAUCE:

1   cup (240 ml) reserved bourbon short rib braising liquid (page 128)

½   cup (120 ml) Beef Stock (page 20)

Salt and freshly ground black pepper

FOR THE GARNISHES:

About ½ cup (70 g) Pea Puree (page 90)

Pea tendrils

Radish microgreens

Shaved Parmesan cheese

with a slightly dampened clean kitchen towel. Repeat with the remaining dough, laying a sheet of plastic wrap between each finished pasta sheet before adding the next, ending with a damp towel on top.

Fill the ravioli: Line a baking sheet with parchment paper and dust it with semolina flour. Lay one pasta sheet onto your work surface and make two rows down the pasta sheet of 1-tablespoon portions of filling, setting them diagonally in a zigzag-like pattern and leaving 1 inch (2.5 cm) of space around each mound of filling. Dip your finger into a small bowl of water and run your wet finger around the edges of the filling to help the pasta stick together. Place a second sheet of pasta on top of the filling, very gently stretching the dough to reach and meet the edges of the bottom pasta sheet. Carefully work your way down the sheet and around each ravioli, sealing in the filling as you go. It is important to get out all of the air in the filling pocket so the ravioli don't explode when cooking. Using a 3-inch (7.5-cm) round cutter, cut out the ravioli and place onto the baking sheet. Cover with plastic wrap and place them in the refrigerator until ready to cook.

Make the horseradish cream: In a blender, combine the crème fraîche, horseradish, and lemon juice and blend on high speed until smooth. Season with salt and white pepper. Transfer the cream to a squeeze bottle and set it aside until ready to serve.

Make the bourbon braising sauce: In a large skillet, combine the braising liquid and stock and cook over high heat until the mixture reduces by two-thirds. Season it with salt and pepper. Set aside the sauce until you are ready to cook the ravioli.

Cook the ravioli: Place a large pot of salted water over high heat and bring it to a rolling boil. Add 10 ravioli and cook for 2 minutes, or until the ravioli begin to float. While the ravioli are cooking, reheat the braising sauce over medium heat until simmering. Add the ravioli to the skillet and cook them in the sauce, basting for 30 seconds to lightly coat the pasta, then use a slotted spoon to remove them to plates. Spoon some of the sauce over the ravioli. Repeat with the remaining ravioli.

To serve: Place 3 to 5 ravioli in the center of each plate and drizzle with more of the braising sauce. Squeeze a small dot of the horseradish cream on top of each raviolo, follow with several quarter- and dime-size dots of pea puree, and top with some pea tendrils, radish microgreens, and shaved Parmesan.

Sweetbread Tortellini

with Mushrooms in Mushroom Broth

They may be offal, but if you cook sweetbreads properly, this meat can be incredibly delicious, especially when stuffed into tortellini! This recipe is another modern spin on a traditional Italian pasta dish, and it also covers two *MasterChef* challenges that I did not have to cook in: the Offal Challenge, as a reward for winning the $20 Mystery Box, and Chef Ramsay's Lobster Tortellini Replication Challenge. The recipe makes about 4 dozen tortellini, so there will be plenty left over to freeze for future meals.

▶ SERVES 4 TO 6 ◀

Make the sweetbread filling: Place the sweetbreads in a large bowl, pour the milk over them, and cover with plastic wrap. Refrigerate them overnight (this removes any impurities or blood that remain in the sweetbreads).

Fill a large bowl with ice and water to create an ice water bath. Place a large pot of salted water over high heat and bring it to a boil. Strain the sweetbreads from the milk, place them in the boiling water, and cook for 2 minutes, then drain and immediately plunge them into the ice bath to stop cooking. Drain.

Use a small paring knife or kitchen scissors to remove the outer membranes and any stringy ligaments from the sweetbreads. Separate the sweetbreads into approximately 1-inch (2.5-cm) sections. Spread ½ cup (65 g) of the flour out over a plate, season it with salt and pepper, and coat the sweetbreads in the flour.

Heat a large cast-iron skillet over high heat and add the oil. Reduce the heat to medium-high, add the sweetbreads, and cook for about 3 minutes on each side, until browned and tender throughout. Remove the sweetbreads from the skillet and set them aside on a plate to cool.

In the bowl of a food processor fitted with the blade attachment, combine the sweetbreads,

FOR THE SWEETBREAD FILLING:

- 1 pound (455 g) veal sweetbreads
- 2 cups (480 ml) whole milk
- ½ cup plus 2 tablespoons (80 g) all-purpose flour
- Salt and freshly ground black pepper
- 3 tablespoons extra-virgin olive oil
- 1 cup (240 ml) mascarpone cheese, at room temperature
- ¼ cup (13 g) finely chopped fresh flat-leaf parsley
- 1 tablespoon finely grated lemon zest
- 1 tablespoon fresh lemon juice

PASTA DOUGH (SEE PAGE 66)

FOR THE MUSHROOM BROTH:

- 2 tablespoons extra-virgin olive oil
- 1 large shallot, minced
- 3 cloves garlic, minced
- 1 pound (455 g) fresh baby bella mushrooms, sliced (reserve about ½ cup/45 g of the best slices for garnish)
- 8 ounces (225 g) fresh shiitake mushrooms, sliced ¼ inch (6 mm) thick
- 2 tablespoons sherry vinegar
- Salt and freshly ground black pepper

FOR THE GARNISHES:

- 1 tablespoon extra-virgin olive oil
- Reserved mushroom slices (see above)
- 1 tablespoon unsalted butter
- Salt and freshly ground black pepper
- Chopped fresh flat-leaf parsley
- Small celery leaves
- White truffle oil (optional)

mascarpone, parsley, lemon zest, lemon juice, and the remaining 2 tablespoons flour and season with salt and pepper. Process until the ingredients are combined, about 30 seconds. Transfer the filling into a piping bag fitted with a ½-inch (12-mm) open tip and refrigerate until the pasta dough is ready.

Make the pasta: Line a baking sheet with parchment paper and sprinkle it generously with semolina flour. Lightly dust the work surface with semolina flour. Cut off one quarter of the pasta dough and wrap the remaining dough in plastic wrap. Dust the dough lightly with flour and flatten it out with your hands into a rectangle. Roll the pasta through the thickest setting of your pasta machine twice, continuing to flour the dough to prevent sticking, as needed. Set the machine to the next lowest setting and repeat the rolling process until you reach the next to lowest setting. You should be able to see through the pasta sheet, but it should not tear. If the pasta becomes too long to handle, slice it in half. Once the pasta sheet is rolled out, dust it lightly with semolina flour, set it onto the baking sheet, and cover with a slightly dampened clean kitchen towel. Repeat with the remaining dough, laying a sheet of plastic wrap between each finished pasta sheet before adding the next, ending with a damp towel on top.

Using a 3-inch (7.5-cm) round cutter, cut out circles from one sheet of pasta. Pipe about 1 teaspoon of filling into each round. Dip your finger in a small bowl of water and run your finger over one side of the round. Fold the tortellini in half to seal the edges, then hold the pasta between your pinky finger and ring finger, wrap the bottom edges around your pinky, and lightly squeeze the pasta together where the points meet. Slide the tortellini off your finger and place it on a baking sheet dusted with semolina flour. Once you have made about 10 tortellini, sprinkle a little semolina flour over them. Repeat until you've used up all the pasta dough and filling. Cover with plastic wrap and refrigerate them until ready to cook. Extra tortellini can be stored in a freezer bag (freeze them flat on a baking sheet until firm before adding them to the bag so they don't stick together) and kept frozen for up to 1 month.

Make the mushroom broth: In a large skillet over medium-high heat, warm the oil. Add the shallot and garlic and cook for about 2 minutes, until lightly browned. Add the mushrooms and cook for 8 to 10 minutes, until lightly browned. Add the vinegar and cook for 1 minute, stirring with a wooden spoon to release any browned bits from the bottom of the pan. Add 4 cups (960 ml) water, season with salt and pepper, and bring to a simmer. Continue to cook for about 15 minutes, until reduced to 2½ cups (600 ml). The broth should only thicken slightly and remain thin.

Make the mushroom garnish: While the broth is cooking, heat the oil for the garnish in a small skillet over medium-high heat. Add the reserved ½ cup (45 g) mushrooms and cook until lightly browned, about 5 minutes. Add the butter and cook, stirring, until melted. Season with salt and pepper and set aside.

Cook the tortellini: Place a large pot of salted water over high heat and bring it to a rolling boil. Add 8 to 10 tortellini and cook for 2 minutes, or until the tortellini begin to float. While the tortellini are cooking, reheat the broth over low heat until simmering. Add the tortellini to the broth as they finish cooking.

To serve: Pour ½ cup (120 ml) broth in the bottom of each large bowl and place 5 to 7 tortellini in each with the rounded edges facing out. Arrange the roasted mushrooms around the tortellini, sprinkle some parsley and celery leaves over the top, and drizzle with a little truffle oil, if using.

Roasted Garlic and Mushroom Risotto

This dish marks the beginning of my love affair with roasted garlic, and it is my best friend, Ryan's, favorite dish. When he hears it's risotto night, he comes running. Actually, he and my godson, Marco, are almost always at my place for dinner, though he never seems to do any damn dishes! The mushrooms suck up a lot of stock going into the risotto, so I call for a little more stock than in the typical risotto. I went with a combination of chanterelles and cremini mushrooms, but really you can use any type of mushrooms. Morels are a nice choice when you can get your hands on them.

■■■➤ SERVES 4 ◀■■■

Make the risotto: In a medium saucepan, bring the stock to a simmer over medium-high heat. Reduce the heat to very low and keep it at a low simmer while you make the risotto.

In a large, heavy-bottomed saucepan, heat the oil over medium-high heat. Add the shallots and cook, stirring frequently, for about 2 minutes, until lightly colored. Squeeze in the roasted garlic and mash it in with the shallots as you stir. Season with salt and pepper. Add the rice and toast it, stirring constantly, for about 3 minutes, until the rice is pale golden in color. Pour in the wine and vinegar and stir to deglaze the pan, then continue cooking until the liquid is reduced by half, about 5 minutes. Add the mushrooms and 1 cup (240 ml) of the hot stock and bring it to a simmer. Reduce the heat to medium and cook, stirring constantly, for about 8 minutes, until the stock is absorbed. Add another ½ cup (120 ml) of the hot stock and continue cooking, stirring constantly, until

(recipe continues)

FOR THE RISOTTO:

3   cups (720 ml) Chicken Stock (page 20)

2   tablespoons extra-virgin olive oil

2   shallots, finely minced

1   head Roasted Garlic (page 16)

Salt and freshly ground black pepper

1   cup (190 g) Arborio rice

½   cup (120 ml) dry white wine, such as Pinot Grigio

1   tablespoon sherry vinegar

4   ounces (115 g) fresh cremini mushrooms, quartered

¼   cup (25 g) finely grated Parmesan cheese

2   tablespoons finely chopped fresh flat-leaf parsley

1   teaspoon finely grated lemon zest

FOR THE PAN-ROASTED MUSHROOMS:

2   tablespoons extra-virgin olive oil

4   ounces (115 g) small fresh chanterelle mushrooms

4   ounces (115 g) fresh cremini mushrooms, quartered

2   tablespoons sherry vinegar

2   tablespoons finely chopped fresh flat-leaf parsley

1   teaspoon finely grated lemon zest

2   tablespoons unsalted butter

Salt and freshly ground black pepper

FOR THE GARNISHES:

Small fresh flat-leaf parsley leaves

Shaved Parmesan cheese

Micro arugula

Finely grated lemon zest

the liquid is absorbed. Repeat with another ½ cup (120 ml) of the hot stock. At this point, taste the risotto for doneness about every 2 minutes. You're looking for the risotto to be creamy looking and al dente, not too thick and never gummy, and it should move around in the pan easily. If the risotto is not yet done, continue to cook by adding ¼ cup (60 ml) of hot stock at a time and stirring constantly until it is absorbed. Add the cheese, parsley, and lemon zest and stir well to combine. Season with salt and pepper.

Make the pan-roasted mushrooms: When the risotto is nearly done, heat a large cast-iron skillet over high heat to almost smoking. Add the oil, then add the mushrooms, reduce the heat to medium-high, and cook for 5 to 7 minutes, stirring frequently, until the mushrooms are softened and lightly browned. Add the vinegar and cook for 1 minute, stirring to release any browned bits from the bottom of the pan. Add the parsley, lemon zest, and butter and toss well to melt the butter and coat the mushrooms. Season with salt and pepper.

To serve: Divide the risotto among large shallow bowls and spoon the pan-roasted mushrooms on top. Garnish each with small parsley leaves, shaved cheese, micro arugula, and a pinch of lemon zest.

Squid Ink Risotto

Squid ink is intensely fishy when it's raw, but something magical happens to it when it is cooked: It transforms into a silky, savory, delicious black coating for pasta and risotto. You can ask your fishmonger to get squid ink for you or order it online.

SERVES 4

Make the risotto: In a medium saucepan, bring the stock to a simmer over medium-high heat. Reduce the heat to very low and keep it at a low simmer while you make the risotto.

In a large, heavy-bottomed saucepan, heat the oil over medium-high heat. Add the shallots and cook, stirring frequently, for about 2 minutes, until lightly colored. Squeeze in the roasted garlic and mash it in with the shallots as you stir. Season with salt and pepper. Add the rice and toast it, stirring constantly, for about 3 minutes, until the rice is pale golden in color. Pour in the wine and vinegar and stir to deglaze the pan, then continue cooking until the liquid is reduced by half, about 5 minutes. Add 1 cup (240 ml) of the hot stock and the squid ink and bring it to a simmer. Reduce the heat to medium and cook, stirring constantly, for about 8 minutes, until the stock is absorbed. Add another ½ cup (120 ml) of the hot stock and continue cooking, stirring constantly, until the liquid is absorbed. Repeat with another ½ cup (120 ml) of the hot stock. At this point, taste the risotto for doneness about every 2 minutes. You're looking for the risotto to be creamy looking and al dente, not too thick and never gummy, and it should move around in the pan easily. If the risotto is not yet done, continue to cook by adding ¼ cup (60 ml) of hot stock at a time and stirring constantly until it is absorbed. Stir in the cheese and season with salt and pepper.

To serve: Divide the risotto among large shallow bowls and garnish each with some shaved Parmesan, parsley, and lemon zest.

FOR THE SQUID INK RISOTTO:

2½ cups (600 ml) Shellfish Stock (page 21)

2 tablespoons extra-virgin olive oil

2 shallots, finely minced

½ head Roasted Garlic (page 16)

Salt and freshly ground black pepper

1 cup (190 g) Arborio rice

½ cup (120 ml) dry white wine, such as Pinot Grigio

2 tablespoons sherry vinegar

1 teaspoon squid ink

¼ cup (25 g) finely grated Parmesan cheese

FOR THE GARNISHES:

Shaved Parmesan cheese

Finely chopped fresh flat-leaf parsley

Finely grated lemon zest

SEAFOOD

When it comes to seafood, living near the water has its advantages, but so does living in Vegas! As a food capital, there are cargo planes full of the freshest products from around the world arriving daily, and very rarely do I go to my fishmonger or Asian market and not find exactly what I'm looking for. Seafood is a perfect canvas to create big flavors, and it is also the most difficult to get right, as once seafood is overcooked, you lose the beautiful texture and subtle flavors that make it so deliciously delicate. Don't be shy to ask your local fishmonger what the freshest selection is, because seafood is one place you do not want to cut corners with quality.

In my house, seafood is a staple, and here I've showcased some of my absolute favorites while giving you a wide variety of flavors and maybe introducing you to some new techniques, such as with my Salt-Baked Red Snapper (page 95). Given that Asian cuisines are heavily based on seafood, my mind will often go to the flavors of Asia, such as with my Spicy Miso Black Cod (page 93) or my Seared Sesame Tuna (page 88). The possibilities for cooking seafood are infinite, so get familiar with my recipes, then go off and explore the oceans through your kitchen.

Smoky San Francisco Cioppino

One of the things I've loved about being a DJ is all the traveling it involves, and the place I find myself going back to most often is San Francisco. I adore the city, from the food to the architecture, and the surrounding areas like Napa Valley excite me with their amazing produce. My love affair with San Fran inspired me to put my own spin on the city's signature dish, cioppino, using fresh shellfish and firm white fish cooked in a deliciously smoky tomato broth. I use orange roughy for the fish, but feel free to substitute any firm flaky white fish that's available in your area.

➡ SERVES 4 ⬅

In a large, tall, lidded pot, heat the oil over medium-high heat. Add the onion, carrots, and celery, season with salt, and cook for about 5 minutes, until softened. Add the roasted garlic, jalapeño and serrano chiles, roasted bell pepper, and ancho chiles and cook, stirring often, for 5 minutes. Add the tomato paste and achiote paste and cook, stirring, for 3 minutes to brown the paste. Add the stock, tomato puree, and liquid smoke. Season with salt and pepper, bring it to a boil, then reduce the heat and simmer for 30 minutes.

Strain the liquid, discard the solids, wipe out the pot, and return the liquid to the pot. Bring it to a simmer over medium-high heat. Add the clams, cover the pan, and cook, shaking the pan, for 1 minute. Add the mussels, cover again, and cook, shaking the pan, for

FOR THE CIOPPINO:

3   tablespoons extra-virgin olive oil

1   medium yellow onion, diced

2   carrots, diced

2   stalks celery, diced

Salt and freshly ground black pepper

5   cloves Roasted Garlic (page 16)

1   jalapeño chile, minced

1   serrano chile, minced

1   red bell pepper, roasted (see page 18) and diced

2   dried ancho chiles, toasted (page 16), stemmed, seeded, and torn into pieces

2   tablespoons tomato paste

1   tablespoon achiote paste (if unavailable, use another 1 tablespoon tomato paste)

3   cups (600 ml) Chicken Stock (page 20) or Seafood Stock (page 21)

1   (28-ounce/785-g) can tomato puree

Couple dashes of liquid smoke

1   pound (455 g) Manila clams, cleaned

1   pound (455 g) mussels, cleaned

1   pound (455 g) medium shell-on shrimp

1   pound (455 g) orange roughy, cut into large chunks

FOR THE GARNISHES:

¼ cup (13 g) chopped fresh flat-leaf parsley

Grated zest of 1 lemon

1   lemon, cut into 4 wedges

1   sourdough baguette

1 more minute. Add the shrimp and fish, cover, and cook for about 3 minutes, until the clams and mussels have opened and the shrimp and fish are cooked through. Discard any clams or mussels that didn't open. Taste the broth and season with salt and pepper if needed.

To serve, divide the clams, mussels, shrimp, and fish among bowls and ladle the broth into the bowls. Top each bowl with some of the parsley and lemon zest and place a lemon wedge on the side. Finish by tearing pieces of baguette over the bowls, keeping more on hand for sopping up the juices at the end.

Citrus and Herb-Stuffed Grilled Branzino

Cooking branzino whole with the skin on enables the delicate fish to hold up to the high heat of the grill. I always buy branzino whole, even if I am making a dish that just calls for the fillets, as it's so much fresher when you get it that way. A sauce with Asian flavors accompanies my stuffed branzino, but you could also try it with my Lemon Beurre Blanc (see page 95). I like to serve this dish with black rice cooked in Shellfish Stock (page 21) or Vegetable Stock (page 19) rather than water, for a big burst of flavor. If branzino is unavailable, you may substitute trout.

SERVES 4

Make the stuffed branzino: Preheat a grill to as hot as you can possibly get it. Alternatively, heat a large skillet or two over medium-high heat.

Season the inside cavities of the fish with salt and pepper and stuff each fish with an equal amount of orange slices, lemon slices, and lime slices (you may have some left over), the parsley, and cilantro. Tie the fish in three evenly spaced spots with butcher's twine. Brush both sides of the fish with oil to prevent sticking. Grill the fish for about 5 minutes on each side, until it feels firm to the touch. Move the branzino to a wire rack set over a baking sheet or a plate to rest while you make the sauce.

Make the garlic-scallion sauce: While the grill is still hot, place the scallions on the grill (or in the skillet), and cook, turning often with tongs, until charred all over, 3 to

(recipe continues)

FOR THE CITRUS AND HERB-STUFFED BRANZINO:

4 whole branzini (1½ to 2 pounds/ 680 to 910 g each), cleaned

Salt and freshly ground black pepper

½ orange, thinly sliced into half moons

½ lemon, thinly sliced into half moons

½ lime, thinly sliced into half moons

8 sprigs fresh parsley

4 sprigs fresh cilantro

Extra-virgin olive oil

FOR THE GARLIC-SCALLION SAUCE:

3 scallions, trimmed

3 cloves Roasted Garlic (page 16)

2 Thai red chiles, finely minced

2 tablespoons finely chopped fresh cilantro

1 tablespoon grated fresh ginger

1 tablespoon toasted sesame oil

½ cup (120 ml) soy sauce

1 tablespoon sambal oelek (chili-garlic paste)

2 tablespoons fresh lime juice

Salt and freshly ground black pepper

FOR THE GARNISHES:

Micro arugula

Finely grated lime zest

Maldon sea salt

5 minutes. Remove from the grill and slice the scallions as thinly as possible.

In a medium bowl, whisk together the roasted garlic, charred scallions, chiles, cilantro, ginger, sesame oil, soy sauce, sambal oelek, and lime juice to combine the ingredients and incorporate the roasted garlic. Season with salt and pepper if needed.

To serve: Remove the twine from each fish and place a whole fish in the center of each plate. If you made black rice, gently place some in a line running down the spine of the fish. Top the fish with garlic-scallion sauce and garnish with micro arugula, lime zest, and a sprinkle of salt.

Chilean Sea Bass

with Bok Choy *and* Orange-Saffron Reduction

Chilean sea bass is a beautiful fish; it's flaky and moist when cooked just right with wonderfully crispy skin, so do yourself a favor and buy this fish skin on. The orange-saffron sauce takes this dish to another level of home cooking. Saffron can be very expensive, so save this dish for a date night or other special occasion to really blow your guests away. Or leave out the saffron for a still amazing everyday meal—either way, this dish is an absolute showstopper.

◄━━━━━━━► SERVES 4 ◄━━━━━━━►

Make the orange-saffron reduction: In a large skillet, heat the oil over medium-high heat. Add the celery, carrot, and shallot and cook, stirring often, for 3 to 5 minutes, until the vegetables are softened. Add the wine and reduce by half, about 10 minutes. Add the stock, saffron, and sugar and reduce again by half, about 10 minutes. Strain the liquid into a bowl, wipe out the pan, and return the reduction to the pan. Add the orange zest and juice, turn the heat to medium-high, and cook for about 5 minutes, until the mixture is reduced to ½ cup (120 ml). Season with salt and pepper and pour the reduction into a bowl for serving.

Make the ginger-lemongrass bok choy: Cut the bok choy in half lengthwise. Pour about 2 inches (5 cm) of water into a large saucepan. Add the ginger, lemongrass, soy sauce, and ponzu sauce and place a steamer basket on top (make sure the surface of the water doesn't touch the basket). Bring the water to a simmer over medium-high heat. Reduce the heat to low, add the bok choy, season with salt and pepper, and steam for 10 minutes, or until the bok choy is tender.

(recipe continues)

FOR THE ORANGE-SAFFRON REDUCTION:

- 2 tablespoons extra-virgin olive oil
- 1 stalk celery, diced
- 1 carrot, diced
- 1 shallot, diced
- 1 cup (240 ml) dry white wine, such as Pinot Grigio
- 1 cup (240 ml) Shellfish Stock (page 21) or Vegetable Stock (page 19)

Pinch of saffron (about 10 threads)

- 1 teaspoon granulated sugar
- ½ teaspoon grated orange zest

Juice of 1 orange

Salt and freshly ground black pepper

FOR THE GINGER-LEMONGRASS BOK CHOY:

- 4 heads baby bok choy
- 1 1-inch (2.5-cm) piece fresh ginger, peeled and sliced
- 1 3-inch (7.5-cm) piece lemongrass (from the bottom), smashed with the back of a knife
- 2 tablespoons soy sauce
- 2 tablespoons ponzu sauce

Salt and freshly ground black pepper

FOR THE CHILEAN SEA BASS:

- 2 tablespoons extra-virgin olive oil
- 4 (6-ounce/170-g, 1-inch-/2.5-cm-thick) skin-on Chilean sea bass fillets

Salt

FOR THE GARNISH:

Radish microgreens

Cook the fish: Meanwhile, heat the oil in a large nonstick skillet until almost smoking. Season the fish with salt, place it in the skillet skin-side down, and cook for 3 to 4 minutes, until the skin is crisp. Flip the fish over and continue cooking for 2 to 3 minutes, until it is firm to the touch but not overcooked. Move the fish to a wire rack placed over a baking sheet or a plate to rest for 3 minutes.

To serve: Spoon about 2 tablespoons of the sauce into the bottom of a shallow bowl. Lay two bok choy halves across each other in almost an X shape and top with the fish, skin-side up. Repeat with the remaining plates. Garnish each with radish microgreens and serve.

Seared Sesame Tuna

with Quail Eggs *and* Wasabi Aioli

Tuna is an incredibly versatile fish eaten all around the world in many different ways, often in raw or semi-raw preparations. Whether it's sushi from Japan or *poke* from Hawaii, it's all delicious in my book! Here, I lightly sear sesame-crusted tuna and serve it with a spicy wasabi aioli and a reduction made with some pretty common Asian ingredients. Then I garnish the dish with sugar snap peas and garlic chives to bring a fresh crunch to the plate. Quail eggs add a little extra creaminess and texture, but if you can't find them, the dish will still be complete without them.

➡ SERVES 4 ◀

Make the soy reduction: In a small, heavy-bottomed skillet, bring the stock to a boil over high heat. Boil for about 10 minutes, until reduced by two thirds. Reduce the heat to medium, add the vinegar, and cook for 2 minutes. Add the fish sauce, hoisin sauce, ponzu sauce, soy sauce, and brown sugar and cook for about 5 minutes, until slightly thickened but still fairly watery. Whisk in the yuzu juice and remove from the heat. Season with salt and pepper. Pour the sauce into a squeeze bottle and set it aside for plating.

Make the sesame tuna: In a small skillet, toast the sesame seeds over medium heat for about 5 minutes, until the white seeds start to darken in color. Remove them from the skillet to a large plate and set aside to cool.

FOR THE SOY REDUCTION:

- 2 cups (480 ml) Chicken Stock (page 20)
- 1 tablespoon rice vinegar
- 1 teaspoon fish sauce
- 1 tablespoon hoisin sauce
- 1 tablespoon ponzu sauce
- 3 tablespoons soy sauce
- 1 tablespoon brown sugar
- 1 teaspoon yuzu juice or fresh lemon juice

Salt and freshly ground black pepper

FOR THE SESAME TUNA:

- 2 tablespoons white sesame seeds
- 2 tablespoons black sesame seeds
- 2 large egg whites
- 4 (6-ounce/170-g) fresh tuna fillets
- 2 tablespoons Japanese togarashi (see Note, page 26; if unavailable, substitute a small amount of cayenne)

Salt and freshly ground black pepper

- 2 tablespoons extra-virgin olive oil

FOR THE GARNISHES:

- 17 sugar snap peas

Olive oil

About 20 garlic chive tips (about 1 inch/2.5 cm long)

- 16 quail eggs

Wasabi Aioli (page 26)

Place the egg whites in a small bowl and beat them until frothy. Place the tuna fillets on a large plate or baking sheet. Gently brush the egg whites over the top of the tuna and sprinkle with half of the togarashi; season with salt and pepper. Invert the tuna fillets into the sesame seeds to coat the egg-washed tops with seeds. Flip the tuna fillets over and return them to the plate; repeat coating them with the remaining egg whites and sesame seeds.

In a large nonstick skillet, heat 1 tablespoon of the oil over medium-high heat until shimmering (test the oil by tossing in a sesame seed; if the oil bubbles around the seed, it's ready). Sear 2 of the fillets for about 1 minute per side (you are really not cooking the tuna here, just searing it on the outside, and the tuna should still be very rare on the inside). Remove the tuna from the skillet to a cutting board and repeat with the remaining oil and tuna fillets. Remove them from the skillet and let the tuna rest for 5 minutes.

Make the garnishes: Remove the peas from the shells of 5 of the sugar snap peas. Bring a medium pot of water to a boil and salt it. Add the remaining 12 sugar snap peas and blanch them for just a few seconds, until slightly softened but still very crisp. Scoop the snap peas out with a slotted spoon and place them on a paper towel–lined plate to dry. Split them in half to expose the peas, trying to keep all the peas on one side. Add the garlic chives to the boiling water and blanch them for a few seconds, until slightly softened but still very crisp. Scoop the garlic chives out with a slotted spoon and put them on another paper towel–lined plate to dry.

To fry the quail eggs, heat a medium nonstick skillet over medium heat and add just enough oil to coat the bottom. Take the point of a sharp paring knife and pierce the top of an egg, then run the knife around the top, removing a portion of the shell, and gently pour the egg into the pan. Quickly repeat with each egg, adding each directly to the pan to fry until done to your liking (fry them in two or three batches).

To serve: Cut the tuna fillets into more or less even rectangles (eat the scraps), then cut the rectangles into 3 or 5 even pieces, depending on the size of the fillet. Arrange the pieces randomly onto plates and drizzle the soy reduction around the plate, roughly 1 tablespoon of sauce per plate. Squeeze out a few varying sized circles of wasabi aioli around the plate, none larger than a dime. Next, place 3 quail eggs around the plate and 1 on top of one of the tuna pieces. Follow that with the sugar snap peas and several individual peas. Finish by randomly arranging the garlic chives on top of and next to the tuna pieces.

Hazelnut and Herb-Crusted Salmon

with Fresh Ricotta *and* Pea Puree

My inspiration for this recipe came from the very last *MasterChef* team battle, where Brandi Mudd and I were teamed up to cook for seventeen of the most influential food critics in the country. While we didn't have to make as many plates as in previous challenges, the stakes were so much higher. Plus, we were feeding people who have literally made and broken careers in the culinary world. Brandi and I decided on a hazelnut-crusted halibut dish that, to our delight, one of the critics described as the essence of spring. Here, I swap in salmon for the halibut and serve it with fresh ricotta and a pea puree—sort of like a deconstructed spring pea and ricotta ravioli.

▶ **SERVES 4** ◀

Make the fresh ricotta: Pour the milk and cream into a large saucepan and stir to combine. Attach a deep-fryer thermometer onto the side of the pan, place over medium-low heat, and bring the mixture to 190°F (88°C), whisking occasionally to prevent scorching on the bottom of the pan. Do not let it boil. Stir in the lemon juice and salt, then remove the pan from the heat and leave it at room temperature for 15 to 20 minutes, until the curds (solids) separate from the whey (liquid). Line a colander or mesh strainer with cheesecloth, scoop the big curds out of the pan with a slotted spoon, and transfer them to the strainer (removing the larger curds first helps keep the liquid from splashing as you pour). Pour the remaining curds and whey into the strainer. Continue draining the ricotta for at least 1 hour and up to 3 hours,

(recipe continues)

FOR THE FRESH RICOTTA:

3   cups (720 ml) whole milk

1   cup (240 ml) heavy cream

3   tablespoons fresh lemon juice

2   teaspoons salt

FOR THE PEA PUREE AND SUGAR SNAP PEA GARNISH:

Salt

8   sugar snap peas

10   ounces (280 g) fresh or thawed frozen peas

¼   cup (13 g) roughly chopped fresh flat-leaf parsley

¼   cup (10 g) roughly chopped fresh cilantro

Freshly ground black pepper

FOR THE HAZELNUT AND HERB-CRUSTED SALMON:

1   cup (135 g) whole hazelnuts

2   tablespoons finely chopped fresh flat-leaf parsley

2   tablespoons finely chopped fresh cilantro

4   (6-ounce/170-g) skin-on salmon fillets

1   large egg white, lightly beaten

Salt and freshly ground black pepper

2   tablespoons extra-virgin olive oil

4   lemon wedges

occasionally pouring out the whey that drips into the bowl. Set aside the ricotta for plating. The ricotta will keep, stored in an airtight container, for up to 1 week in the refrigerator.

Make the pea puree and snap pea garnish:
Bring a medium saucepan of water to a boil and heavily salt it. Add the sugar snap peas and blanch them for just a few seconds, until slightly softened but still very crisp. Scoop the snap peas out with a slotted spoon and place them on a paper towel–lined plate to dry. Return the water to a boil for the peas. Split the snap peas in half to expose the peas, trying to keep all the peas on one side. Set them aside for garnish.

Fill a medium bowl with ice and water to make an ice water bath. Add the 10 ounces (280 g) peas to the blanching water and cook them for about 1½ minutes, until crisp-tender, then add the parsley and cilantro and blanch them for an additional 30 seconds, or until the peas and herbs are softened. Using a slotted spoon, transfer them to the ice water bath, reserving the blanching liquid. Strain the peas and herbs from the water and transfer them to a blender. Add 2 tablespoons of the blanching liquid and blend until smooth and creamy, adding more liquid, 1 tablespoon at a time, if needed. Season with salt and pepper. The pea puree should be firm enough to hold a soft mound, but thin enough to squeeze through a plating bottle. Spoon the mixture into a squeeze bottle for plating (or take out a large spoon to spread the puree).

Make the salmon: In a large skillet over medium heat, toast the hazelnuts for about 5 minutes, shaking the pan often to keep the nuts from burning, until they emit a nutty aroma and are lightly browned. Wrap the nuts in a clean kitchen towel and allow them to rest for 1 minute, then rub the nuts through the towel to remove loose skins (some skins may not come off; that is OK). Allow the nuts to cool, then transfer them to a small food processor and pulse until broken down into approximately ¼-inch (6-mm) pieces. Add the parsley and cilantro and pulse briefly to combine. Turn the nut mixture out onto a baking sheet and shake the pan a bit to create a thick, even layer.

Brush the flesh side of each salmon fillet with egg white and season with salt and pepper. Set the fillets into the nut mixture and press down firmly to ensure an even coating. Invert the salmon onto a plate and refrigerate it for about 15 minutes for the nuts to bond to the salmon.

Heat the oil in a large nonstick skillet over medium heat until sizzling (test the oil by placing a small piece of hazelnut in the oil; if it bubbles around the nut, it is ready). Place the salmon fillets in the skillet crust-side down and cook for 3 minutes, or until the hazelnuts are nicely browned. Flip the salmon over and cook for 2 more minutes, or until the fish skin is nicely browned and the flesh flakes easily.

To plate: Squeeze a circle of the pea puree about 2 inches (5 cm) wide from the squeeze bottle into the middle of each plate. Place a large spoon in a cup of very hot water to warm it, then place the spoon into the ricotta, rotating your wrist all the way to the left and then all the way back to make perfect oval scoops. Set the ricotta onto the center of the pea puree. Place the salmon gently on top of the ricotta and finish by leaning two sugar snap halves against the ricotta. Serve the salmon with the lemon wedges.

Spicy Miso Black Cod

with Fresh Herb Salad

These days, you will find miso cod in one form or another at most Japanese restaurants, but whenever I order it, I feel like it is lacking in spice. So here I borrowed an ingredient from Korea—the fermented chile paste *gochujang*, used widely in the cooking of that country, and that did the trick. The sweet and spicy marinade and sauce are the perfect match for black cod, also known as sablefish, a fish that typically comes from the waters of the North Pacific and that holds up really well to marinades. If it's unavailable, feel free to use regular cod. *Gochujang* is available in Asian food stores.

SERVES 4

Marinate the fish: In a large bowl, whisk together the miso, sake, mirin, sugar, gochujang, yuzu, and vinegar. Transfer ½ cup (120 ml) of the marinade to a small saucepan. Place the cod in the remaining marinade (or place the whole thing in a zip-top bag) and coat the fish well. Place the bowl in the refrigerator to marinate for at least 1 hour or up to 4 hours.

Make the sauce: Place the saucepan with the marinade over medium heat, bring it to a simmer, and cook for 5 minutes, or until reduced by one-quarter. Transfer it to a squeeze bottle and let cool.

Cook the fish: Remove the fish from the marinade and, using paper towels, remove as much of the marinade as possible, paying special attention to the skin. Place the fillets skin-side up on a wire rack set over a baking sheet and let them air-dry for 30 minutes.

(recipe continues)

FOR THE SPICY MISO BLACK COD:

¾ cup (180 g) white miso paste

⅓ cup (75 ml) sake

⅓ cup (75 ml) mirin

¼ cup (50 g) granulated sugar

¼ cup (60 ml) gochujang

1½ teaspoons yuzu juice or fresh lemon juice

1½ teaspoons rice vinegar

4 (6-ounce/170-g) skin-on black cod fillets

2 tablespoons extra-virgin olive oil

FOR THE FRESH HERB SALAD:

3 scallions, thinly sliced on a bias

½ cup (25 g) torn fresh flat-leaf parsley leaves

½ cup (20 g) torn fresh cilantro leaves

½ cup (40 g) purple and green radish microgreens

½ cup (40 g) micro arugula

1 tablespoon fresh lemon juice

1 teaspoon toasted sesame oil

Salt and freshly ground black pepper

FOR THE GARNISHES:

Maldon sea salt

Finely grated lemon zest

Heat the oil in a large nonstick skillet over high heat until almost smoking. Cook the fillets skin-side down for 3 minutes, or until the skin is nice and crispy. Flip the fillets and continue cooking for 1 minute, or until they are cooked through and slightly firm to the touch.

Make the fresh herb salad: In a medium bowl, combine the scallions, parsley, cilantro, radish microgreens, and micro arugula and toss lightly to combine. In a small bowl, whisk together the lemon juice and sesame oil to combine, then season with salt and pepper. Do not dress the salad.

To plate: Place a line of salad about ½ inch (12 mm) wide running the length of each plate. Drizzle each salad with 1 teaspoon of the dressing. Place a black cod fillet next to the salad and sprinkle it with a small pinch of Maldon salt. Squeeze small dots of the miso sauce around the plate and sprinkle a little lemon zest over the salad.

Salt-Baked Red Snapper

FOR THE RED SNAPPER:

5   large egg whites

1   (3-pound/1.4-kg) box kosher salt

1   (2-pound/910-g) whole red snapper, cleaned

¼   lemon, thinly sliced into half moons

¼   lime, thinly sliced into half moons

¼   orange, thinly sliced into half moons

2   sprigs fresh parsley

2   sprigs fresh cilantro

FOR THE LEMON BEURRE BLANC:

1   tablespoon extra-virgin olive oil

1   large shallot, minced

4   cloves garlic, minced

1   cup (240 ml) dry white wine, such as Pinot Grigio

Zest of 1 lemon

2   tablespoons fresh lemon juice

5   tablespoons (2½ ounces/70 g) unsalted butter

Salt and freshly ground black pepper

At first glance, this may seem to call for an insane amount of salt, but there's a method behind the madness: The salt is used to create a barrier to seal in the moisture of the fish, and you won't actually be eating it all. If you're someone who can't eat fish without crispy skin, this may not be the recipe for you, though; because the skin doesn't come in direct contact with the heat, it doesn't have an opportunity to crisp up. But what it lacks in crispiness, it more than makes up for in flavor, and it makes an impressive presentation served family style on a large platter with a beautiful lemon beurre blanc alongside. To get the full dramatic effect of this dish, bring the fish tableside and break open the salt crust in front of your dining companion.

➤ SERVES 2 ◄

Make the snapper: Preheat the oven to 450°F (230°C) and line a baking sheet with a silicone mat or parchment paper.

In a large bowl, beat the egg whites until slightly foamy, about 1 minute. Add the salt and mix well to combine. Pat the snapper dry with paper towels, then stuff the cavity with the lemon, lime, and orange slices and the parsley and cilantro.

Spread a roughly ½-inch (12-mm) layer of salt onto the prepared baking sheet in the shape of the fish to serve as a bed for the fish. Place the fish on the salt bed and cover the fish with the remaining salt, making sure not to leave any gaps. Using your fingers, pat down the salt to seal in the fish. Bake it for about 30 minutes, until the salt crust has developed a very hard shell.

(recipe continues)

Make the lemon beurre blanc: While the fish is cooking, in a large skillet, heat the oil over medium-high heat. Add the shallot and cook for 2 minutes, or until lightly browned. Add the garlic and cook for an additional 1 minute, stirring often. Pour in the wine, bring it to a simmer, and reduce the liquid by three-quarters, about 10 minutes. Add the lemon zest and lemon juice and continue cooking for 1 minute. Strain the sauce into a bowl and wipe out the skillet. Return the sauce to the skillet over low heat and whisk in 1 tablespoon of butter at a time to thicken the beurre blanc. Season with salt and pepper. Pour it into a bowl or gravy boat for serving.

To serve: Remove the fish from the oven and let it sit for 5 minutes. Gently rap around the edges of the salt crust with a metal spoon and lift it off. Wipe off any excess salt from the fish. Move it to a large platter and serve it with the beurre blanc on the side.

POULTRY

As chicken is by far the most widely eaten poultry in this country, most of the recipes in this chapter are made with chicken. I did, however, want to introduce you to a couple of birds you may have never tried before: duck and quail. With the exception of the New-School Duck à l'Orange (page 112), the recipes in this chapter are the easiest to prepare in this book, with a focus on the family weeknight dinner, but with an eye for making them into something special.

I prefer to purchase a whole bird and break it down myself; doing it this way is much cheaper, especially when you save the carcass to make chicken stock afterward. If you have never butchered a whole chicken before, you'll find numerous instructional videos online to guide you. Breaking down a whole chicken gets you a little closer to your food and will help you appreciate what you are cooking a little more. During my time on *MasterChef*, I didn't get a chance to work with chicken, or any other birds for that matter, so I'm extra happy to share my tried-and-true poultry recipes with you here in this book.

Stuffed Bacon-Wrapped Quail

with Pearl Barley Risotto *and* Carrot Puree

When I was young, my dad would tell me stories of going quail and pheasant hunting with his brothers when he was a kid, so I came up with this recipe to honor that part of my father's life. I doubt this is the way my grandmother would have prepared the bounty from the hunt, but I think they all would have enjoyed my spin on cooking this game bird. During the show, Christina Tosi would say, "If it grows together, it goes together." Since 80 percent of a quail's diet is made up of seeds and grains, my pearl barley risotto takes that concept a step further: "If it eats it, I will eat it with it."

━━━━━━▶ **SERVES 4** ◀━━━━━━

Make the quail: Preheat the oven to 500°F (260°C) and line a baking pan with foil.

Place the ricotta in a fine-mesh strainer over a bowl. Place it in the refrigerator to drain for at least 1 hour or up to overnight.

Lightly brush the quail with oil and season it with salt and pepper inside and out. Remove the ricotta from the refrigerator and season it with salt and pepper. Stuff each quail with one quarter of the ricotta mixture, loosely tie the legs together with kitchen twine, and place them in the freezer for 10 minutes to firm up the ricotta (or refrigerate for up to a day). Wrap the bacon around the birds, starting at the breast and extending behind the wings (the wings should be exposed rather than wrapped under the bacon), with the ends meeting underneath the bird.

(recipe continues)

1 cup (240 ml) ricotta cheese

4 semi-boneless quail

Extra-virgin olive oil

Salt and freshly ground black pepper

2 slices bacon, cut in half lengthwise

FOR THE PEARL BARLEY RISOTTO:

3 to 4 cups (720 to 960 ml) Chicken Stock (page 20)

2 tablespoons extra-virgin olive oil

1 shallot, minced

2 cloves Roasted Garlic (page 16)

1 cup (200 g) pearl barley

½ cup (120 ml) dry white wine, such as Pinot Grigio

2 tablespoons unsalted butter

¼ cup (25 g) grated Parmesan cheese

FOR THE CARROT PUREE:

2 cups (480 ml) whole milk

1 cup (240 ml) heavy cream

4 large carrots, roughly chopped

Salt and freshly ground white pepper

FOR THE GARNISH:

Carrot tops

Place the quail in the prepared pan breast-side up and roast them for about 15 minutes, until the bacon is starting to crisp and the quail is just cooked through. Remove from the oven and let rest for 5 minutes.

Make the risotto: While the quail is in the oven, in a medium saucepan, bring the stock to a simmer over medium-high heat. Reduce the heat to very low and keep it at a low simmer while you make the risotto.

In a large skillet, heat the oil over medium-high heat. Add the shallot and cook, stirring frequently, for about 2 minutes, until lightly colored. Squeeze in the roasted garlic and mash it in with the shallot. Season with salt and pepper. Add the barley and toast it, stirring constantly, for about 3 minutes, until pale golden in color. Add the wine and stir to deglaze the pan, then continue cooking until the liquid is absorbed, about 5 minutes.

Add 1 cup (240 ml) of the hot stock and bring it to a simmer. Reduce the heat to medium and cook, stirring constantly, for about 8 minutes, until the stock is absorbed. Add another 1 cup (240 ml) of the hot stock and continue cooking, stirring constantly, until the liquid is absorbed. Repeat with another ½ cup (120 ml) of the hot stock. At this point, taste the risotto for doneness about every

2 minutes. You're looking for the risotto to be slightly softened but more al dente than rice risotto. If the risotto is not yet done, continue to cook by adding ¼ cup (60 ml) of hot stock at a time and stirring constantly until it is absorbed. Stir in the butter and cheese and season with salt and pepper.

Make the carrot puree: While the risotto is cooking, in a medium saucepan, combine the milk and cream over medium-high heat and bring them to a simmer. Add the carrots and season fairly heavily with salt and white pepper. Reduce the heat to medium and cook for about 15 minutes, until the carrots are tender. Strain the carrots through a mesh strainer, reserving about 1 cup (240 ml) of the cooking liquid (you probably won't need the entire cup). Place the carrots and ¼ cup (60 ml) of the liquid into a blender and blend on high speed until very smooth, adding more of the cooking liquid as needed.

To serve: Place some of the carrot puree in the middle of four serving plates and gently spread it with the back of a spoon into a small circle. Scoop the risotto with a large spoon onto one side of the puree, leaving half uncovered. Finish by placing the quail on top of the risotto and garnish with some carrot tops.

Chicken Saltimbocca Sandwich

As part of my mission of elevating how we cook at home, I wanted to share with you an incredibly delicious sandwich that is also very easy to make. A super-fresh spicy lemon aioli that can be pulled together in under ten minutes makes chicken saltimbocca into a high-end restaurant-quality sandwich. Wrap your sandwiches up, bring them on your next picnic or day at the beach, and throw in a bag of salt and vinegar chips, my personal favorite, to enjoy with them.

SERVES 4

Make the spicy lemon aioli: Fill a small bowl with ice and water to make an ice water bath. Bring a small pot of water to a rolling boil over high heat and salt the water. Lower the egg into the water; cover, reduce the heat to medium, and cook for exactly 6 minutes with the lid on. Remove the egg from the water and place it in the ice water bath; let it cool completely, then peel it. In a blender, combine the soft-boiled egg, lemon zest, lemon juice, vinegar, and cayenne and blend to combine. With the blender on low speed, very slowly drizzle in the oil through the feed tube to thicken the aioli to a creamy consistency. Season with salt and pepper and transfer it to a squeeze bottle for plating (if you don't have a squeeze bottle, use a small spoon to top the chicken with aioli). Set it aside while you prepare the chicken.

Make the chicken saltimbocca: Preheat the oven to 350°F (175°C).

(recipe continues)

FOR THE SPICY LEMON AIOLI:

1   large egg

Grated zest of 1 lemon

3   tablespoons fresh lemon juice

1   teaspoon white wine vinegar

½   teaspoon ground cayenne

1   cup (240 ml) extra-virgin olive oil

Salt and freshly ground black pepper

FOR THE CHICKEN SALTIMBOCCA:

2   boneless, skinless chicken breasts

½   cup (65 g) all-purpose flour

1   tablespoon salt

1   tablespoon freshly ground black pepper

½   teaspoon ground cayenne

1   teaspoon dried oregano

1   teaspoon dried rosemary

4   tablespoons (60 ml) extra-virgin olive oil

4   slices prosciutto

8   slices provolone cheese

4   ciabatta buns, buttered and toasted

Baby arugula

Butterfly each chicken breast and cut each in half to make four pieces, removing the tenderloins and reserving them for another recipe. Using the flat side of a meat tenderizer, lightly pound out each chicken breast between two sheets of plastic wrap to an even ¼-inch (6-mm) thickness.

In a shallow plate, combine the flour, salt, pepper, cayenne, oregano, and rosemary. Dredge the chicken all over in the flour mixture and set aside. Heat 2 tablespoons of the oil in a large cast-iron pan over high heat until almost smoking. Add two of the chicken breasts and cook for 2 minutes on each side, or until lightly browned and almost cooked through. Place the chicken on a baking sheet. Repeat with the remaining oil and chicken breasts, adding them to the baking sheet. Top each piece of chicken with 1 slice of prosciutto and 2 slices of cheese. Bake them for 5 minutes, or until the cheese is melted.

To serve: Place a piece of chicken on each toasted ciabatta bun bottom, top with a small handful of arugula, and finish with a healthy squeeze of aioli. Top the buns to complete the sandwiches and serve.

Chicken Piccata

This recipe is one that I like to make when I don't feel like working too hard in the kitchen, but still want a dish that's packed full of flavor. It can be completed in under thirty minutes—perfect for putting into your dinner rotation. I love capers, so I go a little crazy with them here, calling for a whole jar! But if you're not as enamored with capers as I am, you can cut back on them or eliminate them completely. Serve with my Roasted Garlic Mashed Potatoes (page 156) to complete the meal.

⟹ SERVES 4 ⟸

Butterfly each chicken breast and cut each in half to make eight pieces, removing the tenderloins and reserving them for another recipe. Using the flat side of a meat tenderizer, lightly pound out each chicken breast between two sheets of plastic wrap to an even ¼-inch (6-mm) thickness.

On a large plate, combine the flour, salt, pepper, cayenne, oregano, thyme, and rosemary. Dredge the chicken breasts completely in the seasoned flour and set them aside on a baking sheet.

Heat 1 tablespoon of the oil in a large nonstick skillet over medium-high heat. Add two of the chicken breasts and cook for about 2 minutes per side, until lightly browned and just cooked through. Transfer them to a baking sheet. Repeat with the remaining oil and chicken, working in three batches. Add the wine to the pan, bring it to a simmer, and cook for 5 minutes, or until the wine is absorbed. Add the stock and bring it to a simmer. Add the capers, lemon juice, parsley, and sugar and stir well to dissolve the sugar. Whisk in the butter 1 tablespoon at a time until melted and a sauce is formed, then return the chicken to the pan to coat it well with the sauce. The pan will be quite full, but that's OK because you're just looking to give the chicken a final light toss with the sauce and heat it through.

4   boneless, skinless chicken breasts

¾   cup (95 g) all-purpose flour

1   tablespoon salt

1   tablespoon freshly ground black pepper

¾   teaspoon ground cayenne

1   tablespoon dried oregano

1   teaspoon dried thyme

1   teaspoon dried rosemary

4   tablespoons (60 ml) extra-virgin olive oil

½   cup (120 ml) dry white wine, such as Pinot Grigio

½   cup (120 ml) Chicken Stock (page 20)

½   cup (55 g) drained capers

¼   cup (60 ml) fresh lemon juice

¼   cup (13 g) chopped fresh flat-leaf parsley

1   teaspoon granulated sugar

¾   stick (3 ounces/85 g) unsalted butter

Herb-Roasted Whole Chicken

with Pan Jus

I love a good grocery store rotisserie chicken as much as the next guy, but the truth is there's a more flavorful way to get your roast chicken fix. This is a great recipe for a weeknight family dinner: Once you have the roasted garlic butter and roasted garlic salt on hand, it doesn't take very long to prep, and then you just throw it in the oven and wait for it to roast. I rub some roasted garlic butter under the skin, which not only keeps the meat juicy, but also imparts a ton of flavor in places your seasoning might not otherwise get to. Serve this chicken with my Au Gratin Potatoes (page 157) or Crazy Cheese Truffle Mac (page 155) for an amazing family dinner.

➤ SERVES 4 ◄

Roast the chicken: Preheat the oven to 375°F (190°C).

Run the chicken under cold water to rinse it, then pat it dry with paper towels. Rub the roasted garlic–rosemary butter pieces under the skin, making sure to slide some down under the skin on the legs and the thighs.

Place the lemon and orange in a large bowl. Add 5 of the rosemary sprigs, 6 of the thyme sprigs, the sage leaves, bay leaves, and oil and season with salt and pepper. Toss to combine the ingredients and coat them in the oil. Stuff the mixture into the cavity of the chicken, then rub the garlic salt into the chicken.

In a roasting pan, combine the carrots, celery, onion, garlic, and stock. Tuck the wings of the chicken underneath the bird and tie the legs together with butcher's twine to help the bird hold its shape. Place the chicken on the vegetables breast-side up and roast it for 1 hour and 15 minutes. Raise the oven temperature

(recipe continues)

FOR THE HERB-ROASTED WHOLE CHICKEN:

- 1 whole chicken (about 4 pounds/ 1.8 kg)
- ½ cup (4 ounces/115 g) Roasted Garlic–Rosemary Butter (page 18), cut into ½-tablespoon pieces
- 1 lemon, halved
- 1 orange, halved
- 6 sprigs fresh rosemary
- 8 sprigs fresh thyme
- 10 sage leaves
- 3 bay leaves
- 3 tablespoons extra-virgin olive oil

Salt and freshly ground black pepper

- 1 tablespoon Roasted Garlic Salt (page 17)
- 3 carrots, cut into large chunks
- 4 stalks celery, cut into large chunks
- 1 large onion, cut into large chunks
- 6 cloves garlic, peeled
- ½ cup (120 ml) Chicken Stock (page 20)

FOR THE PAN JUS:

- 1 cup (240 ml) Chicken Stock (page 20)
- ½ stick (2 ounces/55 g) cold unsalted butter

Salt and freshly ground black pepper

to 400°F (205°C) and continue roasting for 15 minutes more, or until an instant-read thermometer inserted in the breasts and thighs reads 165°F (75°C) and the juices flow clear. Remove from the oven and let it rest for 20 minutes.

Make the pan jus: Strain the juices from the roasting pan into a large skillet, and discard the vegetables. Add the stock, place it over high heat, and bring it to a boil. Boil until reduced by half, about 8 minutes. Turn off the heat and whisk in the butter 1 tablespoon at a time to thicken the sauce. Taste and season with salt and pepper if needed.

To serve: Place the chicken on a serving platter and serve with the pan jus alongside.

Lazy Day Chicken Parmesan

Although my lazy days are now few and far between, I still enjoy making this simple meal to wind down after cooking high-end dishes and doing crazy events all week. It's perfect when I have extra All-Day Red Sauce (page 62) on hand, and I love to serve it alongside my homemade fettuccine (page 64). I rarely use store-bought bread crumbs in my cooking, but for this recipe I make an exception and use Japanese panko, as they bring an extra crunch to the dish.

▶ **SERVES 4** ◀

Preheat the oven to 400°F (205°C).

Cut the chicken breasts in half lengthwise to make four pieces. Place each chicken breast half between two pieces of plastic wrap and, using the flat side of a meat tenderizer, pound the chicken to about ½ inch (12 mm) thick.

On a large plate, combine the flour, thyme, oregano, cayenne, salt, and pepper. In a large, shallow bowl, whisk the eggs, milk, and hot sauce. On another large plate, combine the panko, rosemary, and thyme and season well with salt and pepper.

Lay the chicken onto the flour mixture, then flip it over to completely coat the chicken. Dip the chicken into the egg mixture, making sure to coat the entire breast, then let excess moisture drip off. Move the breasts to the panko mixture and press down to get an even coating of the breading onto each side of the chicken. Place the chicken on a wire rack placed over a baking sheet and freeze it for 30 minutes to firm up the breading.

2   large boneless, skinless chicken breasts

1   cup (125 g) all-purpose flour

1   tablespoon dried thyme

1   tablespoon dried oregano

½   teaspoon ground cayenne

1   tablespoon salt

1   tablespoon freshly ground black pepper

2   large eggs, beaten

½   cup (120 ml) whole milk

3   tablespoons hot sauce

1½ cups (120 g) panko bread crumbs

Leaves from 2 sprigs fresh rosemary, finely chopped

Leaves from 2 sprigs fresh thyme, finely chopped

Salt and freshly ground black pepper

1   quart (960 ml) peanut oil

1⅓ cups (315 ml) All-Day Red Sauce (page 62)

1   pound (455 g) fresh mozzarella cheese, sliced ¼ inch (6 mm) thick

½   cup (50 g) grated Parmesan cheese

Pour the oil into a large high-sided skillet or sauté pan and heat it over medium-high heat to 350°F (175°C). Place the chicken breasts into the oil two at a time and cook for 2 to 3 minutes on each side, until lightly browned. Return the breasts to the wire rack over the baking sheet.

Working carefully to avoid dripping, cover each chicken breast with ⅓ cup of the red sauce and one quarter of the mozzarella cheese. Bake (still on the wire rack) for 5 minutes, then remove the baking sheet from the oven and sprinkle the Parmesan cheese over the chicken breasts. Return to the oven and bake until the cheese is melted and starting to brown, about 5 more minutes, then serve.

New-School Duck à l'Orange

What makes this "new school"? Most of the classic French preparations call for cooking the duck whole, and while I am an advocate for cooking on the bone, I felt there could be a better way of creating the classic flavors for this dish. I still start with a whole bird, but then I remove the breasts and legs and save the carcass to make a deep orange sauce, serve the duck over spicy green beans, and garnish with pea tendrils to add freshness to the dish.

There is no hiding the fact that there are a lot of steps to complete this recipe, but I am confident that once you get past breaking down the duck, you will be able to successfully re-create it. To make the dish easier to accomplish, swap the whole duck for two duck breasts and two duck legs. The recipe serves two generously, with one breast and one leg per person, but you could easily extend it to four servings, with two guests getting the breasts and the other two enjoying the legs.

➤ SERVES 2 TO 4 ◀

Break down the duck: Cut the breasts and legs from the duck and chop the carcass into four pieces. Reserve the carcass, neck, liver, kidneys, and heart for the sauce (if your duck didn't come with the organs, or you are using duck pieces rather than a whole duck, you can make the recipe without them).

Marinate the duck breasts: Peel the rind from 4 of the oranges with a vegetable peeler, then cut the peel into very thin julienne slices. Juice the oranges to make about 1 cup (240 ml). Pour half of the orange juice into a small bowl (save the rest for making the sauce later) and whisk

(recipe continues)

FOR THE DUCK À L'ORANGE:

1   (5-pound/2.3 kg) young duckling
5   oranges
3   tablespoons granulated sugar
1   teaspoon Maldon sea salt, plus more for seasoning
1   teaspoon freshly ground black pepper, plus more for seasoning
2   carrots, roughly chopped
3   shallots, roughly chopped
2   stalks celery, roughly chopped
½   teaspoon black peppercorns
5   sprigs fresh parsley
3   sprigs fresh thyme
1   sprig fresh rosemary
3   bay leaves
2   dried árbol chiles
5   cloves Roasted Garlic (page 16)
4   allspice berries
2   star anise pods
3   tablespoons sherry vinegar
½   cup (120 ml) dry white wine, such as Pinot Grigio
About 3 cups (720 ml) Chicken Stock (page 20) or Vegetable Stock (page 19)
½   stick (2 ounces/55 g) unsalted butter

FOR THE SPICY GREEN BEANS:

8   ounces (225 g) fresh green beans
1   tablespoon extra-virgin olive oil
1   tablespoon sherry vinegar
½   teaspoon red pepper flakes
Salt and freshly ground black pepper

FOR THE GARNISHES:

Pea tendrils
Maldon sea salt

in the sugar, salt, and pepper until the sugar is dissolved. Add half of the julienned orange zest and refrigerate the rest to use for garnish. Using a sharp knife, score the skin of the duck breasts diagonally into a small diamond pattern, taking care not to pierce the meat. Place the breasts in a zip-top bag and pour the orange juice mixture over the breasts. Refrigerate them for at least 4 hours or up to overnight to marinate.

Cook the duck legs: Preheat the oven to 350°F (175°C).

Place the duck legs in a large cast-iron skillet fat-side down and set it over medium-low heat. Cook for about 15 minutes to render the fat from the legs, flipping once at about 10 minutes. If your legs are particularly fatty on the sides, lean them up against the side of the pan and cook for another 5 minutes to render the extra fat. Remove the duck legs to a plate and pour 1 tablespoon of the rendered duck fat into a large Dutch oven or stockpot. In the same skillet, add the duck carcass, neck, liver, kidneys, and heart and cook for about 20 minutes to render the fat from the carcass. Strain out the carcass and organs. Discard the organs, reserving the carcass and duck fat.

Heat the rendered duck fat in the Dutch oven over medium-high heat. Add the carrots and cook for 5 minutes, then add the shallots and celery and cook for another 5 minutes, stirring often. Add the peppercorns, parsley, thyme, rosemary, bay leaves, chiles, roasted garlic, allspice, and star anise and cook for about 3 minutes, until aromatic. Add the vinegar and cook for 2 minutes, stirring to release any browned bits that stuck to the bottom of the pot. Add the wine and cook for about 5 minutes, until reduced by half. Place the duck legs and carcass pieces in the pot, nestling them against each other, and add just enough chicken stock to cover the legs.

Season with salt and pepper (lightly, as you will later be reducing and concentrating the sauce), increase the heat to high, and bring it to a boil. Turn off the heat. Cover, place in the oven, and roast for about 1½ hours, until the meat on the legs is tender. Remove the legs to a wire rack set over a baking sheet and set the oven to broil. Strain the liquid from the pot into a large sauté pan to use for the sauce, discarding the remaining solids.

Make the sauce: Heat the duck leg cooking liquid over medium-high heat and simmer for about 30 minutes, until reduced to about 1 cup (240 ml). Add the reserved orange juice and cook for 5 minutes. Turn off the heat and whisk in the butter 1 tablespoon at a time, until the sauce is thickened. Taste and season with salt and pepper if needed, move to a bowl or small pitcher, and set aside for plating.

Cook the duck breasts: While the sauce is cooking, remove the duck breasts from the marinade and pat them dry with paper towels. Place the duck breasts skin-side down in a cold cast-iron skillet and set it over medium-low heat (starting in a cold pan helps render the fat before crisping the skin). Cook for 10 to 15 minutes, until the fat is rendered, then increase the heat to medium-high and cook for 2 minutes more to crisp the skin. Flip them over and cook for 1 minute more for rare, another minute for medium-rare, then move the duck breasts to a plate to rest.

Finish the duck legs: Place the legs under the broiler and cook them for about 5 minutes, until the skin is crisp. Set aside to rest.

Cook the green beans: While the duck is finishing up, fill a medium bowl with ice and water to make an ice water bath. Bring a large pot of water to a boil and salt it. Blanch the reserved julienned orange peel for 30 seconds, scoop it out with a slotted spoon, and move it to the ice water bath to cool. Scoop the orange peel out and place it on a paper towel–lined plate to dry. Set it aside for plating.

Add the green beans to the same boiling water and blanch them for 2 minutes, or until just starting to soften. Move the green beans to the ice water bath, then drain.

In a medium skillet, heat the oil over high heat. Add the green beans and cook for about 3 minutes, until some of the green beans char in a few places. Add the vinegar and cook for 1 minute, or until almost completely absorbed. Add the red pepper flakes and season with salt and pepper.

To serve: Pour some of the orange sauce into the middle of a plate (ideally one that has a round indention so you can create a perfect circle of sauce). Carefully place a handful of the green beans on top of the sauce. Slice the duck breast ¼ inch (6 mm) thick and lay it on one side of the green beans. Place the leg opposite the breast. Top with the julienned orange peel, a few pea tendrils, and a sprinkle of salt. Repeat with the remaining plates and serve.

MEAT

It's no secret that I am a full-on carnivore, but I choose my meat with care. I always buy my beef, pork, and game from my local butcher, Ron, as I can count on the quality of his meat and he takes pride in providing the absolute best to his customers. The benefits of buying from a dedicated butcher are many. First and foremost, your butcher can tell you exactly where that animal came from, and often they can even tell you what the animal's diet was and at what age it was slaughtered. Most butcher shops buy whole animals and butcher them on site, which means that animal will be at the peak of freshness when you buy it, which translates to better flavor in your cooking.

In this chapter, I show you some of my favorite ways to prepare meat, including how to dry-age a steak at home (see page 137) and make perfectly crispy pork belly (see page 118). And I'll share with you my dad's favorite, the Holiday Rib Roast (page 131). I get weak in the knees when it comes to a perfectly cooked steak; I'll show you my way of throwing a little foie gras into the pan to create an ideal steak dinner. The chapter culminates with my *MasterChef* Finale entree, the dish that Gordon Ramsay said redefined the way venison should be plated and that has become my signature dish. I truly hope you enjoy making these recipes as much as I enjoyed creating them for you.

Crispy Pork Belly

with **Amaretto–Butternut Squash Puree**

Oh, pork belly, pork belly, pork belly! It's just pork belly, people. We Americans love bacon but can be scared off when it goes by the name *belly*, though in fact it is one of the premiere cuts of the pig. For this recipe, Asian flavors were what called to me, as soy and hoisin work perfectly with this fatty cut of meat, but I just couldn't get it quite the way I wanted it. Until I figured out what was missing: sake. The alcohol in the sake helps to break down the pork belly as it cooks, creating an incredibly tender and juicy cut of pork. And searing it in a raging hot skillet finishes the belly with an insanely crispy skin.

SERVES 4 TO 6

Make the crispy pork belly: Preheat the oven to 300°F (150°C).

Heat 1 tablespoon of the oil in a Dutch oven, preferably cast iron, over medium-high heat. Add the shallots and garlic and cook, stirring often, for 2 minutes, or until the shallots begin to color. Add the sake and cook until reduced by half, 5 to 7 minutes. Add 1 cup (240 ml) water, the stock, gochujang, hoisin sauce, sambal oelek, ponzu sauce, soy sauce, vinegar, and brown sugar and bring them to a boil, stirring to dissolve the sugar. Place the pork belly in the liquid, cover, and turn off the heat. Transfer it to the oven and braise for 3 hours.

Make the amaretto-butternut squash puree: While the pork belly is in the oven, line a baking sheet with parchment paper. Place the squash on the sheet, toss it with the oil, and season with salt and pepper. Cover with aluminum foil and roast it for 1 hour, or until the squash is tender, turning it halfway through to cook it evenly.

While the squash is roasting, pour the amaretto into a small skillet over medium-high heat and bring to

FOR THE CRISPY PORK BELLY:

2   tablespoons extra-virgin olive oil

2   shallots, minced

6   cloves garlic, minced

1   cup (240 ml) sake

3   cups (720 ml) Chicken Stock (page 20)

2   tablespoons gochujang (see page 93)

2   tablespoons hoisin sauce

1   tablespoon sambal oelek (chili-garlic paste)

¼   cup (60 ml) ponzu sauce

¼   cup (60 ml) soy sauce

1   tablespoon rice vinegar

3   tablespoons brown sugar

1   (2-pound/920-g) skin-on pork belly

FOR THE AMARETTO-BUTTERNUT SQUASH PUREE:

1   small butternut squash (about 2 pounds/920 g), peeled, seeded, and cut into ½-inch (12-mm) cubes

1   tablespoon olive oil

Salt and freshly ground black pepper

½   cup (120 ml) amaretto

2   tablespoons heavy cream

FOR THE GARNISHES:

Radish microgreens

Pea tendrils

a boil. Boil for about 7 minutes, until reduced by about three-quarters, watching carefully near the end so it doesn't boil over. Turn off the heat, add the cream, and stir to heat through. Place the squash and amaretto mixture in a food processor or blender and blend until very smooth. Season with salt and pepper.

Finish the pork belly: Remove the pork belly from the oven, take the belly out of the cooking liquid, and place it on a wire rack set over a baking sheet to cool and dry a bit. Strain the cooking liquid through a fine-mesh strainer into a large skillet over medium-high heat and bring it to a boil. Boil until reduced by about half, about 30 minutes, to make a liquid sauce.

Cut the pork belly into four or six even rectangular pieces. Heat the remaining 1 tablespoon oil in a large cast-iron skillet over high heat to smoking. Add the pork belly pieces and sear them on all sides for about 1 minute per side and 2 minutes on the skin side, until crisp all over.

To plate: Place about ¼ cup (60 ml) of the butternut squash puree in the middle of each plate and, with the back of a spoon, spread the puree into a circle. Top with one piece of pork belly, drizzle with the sauce, garnish with some radish microgreens and pea tendrils, and serve.

Pork Tenderloin

with Bourbon Reduction *and* Smoked Cheddar Polenta

Every time I cook pork, I think of my dad, an Iowa native to his core. My brother, Tim, is just like him, with a stronger affection for pork than even me (and I'm the one with the pig tattoo). I will say Iowa pork is arguably some of the best pork in the country, and every time my brother would visit my dad, he would head back to Indiana with a cooler full of Iowa pork products. My crew from the *MasterChef* Farmers Team Challenge attempted something similar to this recipe, but we couldn't get our act together and it was a catastrophe. This one is my redemption for the Red Team!

➤ SERVES 4 ◄

Make the pork tenderloin rub: Place the ancho, guajillo, and árbol chiles in the bowl of a small food processor and process until finely ground. There may be small flakes of chile remaining; this is OK. Add the roasted garlic salt, brown sugar, allspice, star anise, and pepper and process until finely ground. Place each tenderloin on a sheet of plastic wrap and use your hands to fully coat them with the rub (wear disposable gloves to keep your hands from coming in contact with the chiles). Tightly wrap each tenderloin in its plastic wrap and refrigerate them for 1 hour.

Make the bourbon reduction: While the pork is in the refrigerator, in a large, heavy-bottomed skillet, heat the oil over medium-high heat. Add the shallots and cook for 5 minutes, or until softened. Add the roasted and fresh garlic and cook, stirring occasionally, for 3 to 4 minutes, until the garlic is browned.

Remove the skillet from the heat and add the bourbon. Return the skillet to medium-high heat, add the vinegar, and cook until the liquid is reduced by one-third,

(recipe continues)

FOR THE PORK TENDERLOIN AND RUB:

- 2 dried ancho chiles, toasted (see page 16), stemmed, and seeded
- 2 dried guajillo chiles, toasted (see page 16), stemmed, and seeded
- 2 dried árbol chiles, toasted (see page 16), stemmed, and seeded
- 3 tablespoons Roasted Garlic Salt (page 17)
- ¼ cup (55 g) packed brown sugar
- 6 allspice berries, toasted
- 2 star anise pods, toasted
- 1 teaspoon freshly ground black pepper
- 2 whole pork tenderloins (about 12 ounces/340 g each)
- 3 tablespoons extra-virgin olive oil
- 2 tablespoons Chile-Lime Butter (page 18)

FOR THE BOURBON REDUCTION:

- 2 tablespoons extra-virgin olive oil
- 2 shallots, roughly chopped
- 4 cloves Roasted Garlic (page 16)
- 4 cloves fresh garlic, roughly chopped
- 1½ cups (360 ml) bourbon
- ¼ cup (60 ml) apple cider vinegar
- 2 dried ancho chiles
- 2 dried guajillo chiles
- 1 dried árbol chile
- 2 canned chipotle chiles in adobo sauce
- 2 cups (480 ml) Chicken Stock (page 20)
- 5 tablespoons (2½ ounces/70 g) cold unsalted butter

Salt

(ingredients continue)

about 10 minutes. Add the ancho, guajillo, árbol, and chipotle chiles, then add the stock and continue to cook until the mixture reduces by two-thirds, about 15 minutes. Strain the reduction through a fine-mesh strainer into a bowl, then pour it into a small saucepan. Place it over low heat and whisk in the butter 1 tablespoon at a time, stirring continuously until all the butter is incorporated and the reduction lightly coats a spoon. Taste and add salt if needed.

Make the smoked Cheddar polenta: While you're making the reduction, pour 3 cups (720 ml) water into a medium saucepan and add the salt. Place it over medium-high heat and bring to a boil. Slowly whisk in the polenta, return it to a simmer, then reduce the heat to medium. Whisk or stir continually until the mixture starts to thicken and pulls away from the sides of the pan, 4 to 6 minutes, adding a small amount of water if the polenta starts getting too thick. Stir in the cheese and season with salt and pepper. Turn off the heat and set it aside until you're ready to serve.

Cook the pork: Place a large cast-iron skillet over high heat and get it smoking hot. Add the oil and swirl it around the pan. Place the tenderloins in the pan and cook for about 3 minutes on each of four sides until they are nicely seared all over. Add the chile-lime butter and baste the tenderloins for about 2 minutes, moving them around in the pan constantly, until an instant-read thermometer inserted into the middle of the thickest end of the tenderloin reads between 145 and 150°F (63 to 66°C). Transfer the tenderloins to a wire rack set over a baking sheet or a cutting board to rest for 8 minutes before slicing.

To serve: Check the consistency of the polenta (it tends to firm up as it sits), and if needed, stir or whisk in a little hot water to thin it to a creamy consistency. Place a large scoop of the polenta in the middle of each plate and, using a large spoon, spread it into a circle. Carefully drizzle some of the bourbon reduction around the base of the polenta to create a ring around it. Cut the pork tenderloin into three 1½-inch- (4-cm-) thick slices and place them onto the middle of each polenta circle. Drizzle the remaining bourbon reduction over the pork, garnish with some micro arugula, and serve.

FOR THE SMOKED CHEDDAR POLENTA:

1   teaspoon salt

1   cup (180 g) fine polenta

8   ounces (225 g) smoked Cheddar cheese, shredded

Salt and freshly ground black pepper

FOR THE GARNISH:

Micro arugula

Rack of Lamb

with Eggplant Puree *and* Red Wine Demi-Glace

When I'm cooking with lamb, my thoughts go to the Mediterranean. I wanted to keep some of those classic flavors in this dish but with a modern American flare, so I added an insanely rich and luxurious red wine demi-glace to tie the dish together. I love to serve this with my Au Gratin Potatoes (page 157) or Roasted Garlic Mashed Potatoes (page 156), or sometimes I'll just make a rack with the demi-glace and call it a day. The roasted garlic marinade can be used on all kinds of meats; two of my favorites are skirt steak and hanger steak. Veal demi-glace can be found in some butcher shops and online.

SERVES 4

Make the roasted garlic marinade: Place the lamb in a large zip-top bag. In the bowl of a small food processor, combine the garlic, 1 cup (240 ml) of the oil, the rosemary, and thyme and season with salt and pepper. Process until the garlic is broken down. Pour the marinade over the lamb, seal the bag, and massage the marinade into the meat. Refrigerate and marinate for at least 1 hour or up to overnight.

Make the rosemary-thyme salt: In the bowl of a small food processor, combine the salt, rosemary, thyme, onion powder, garlic powder, and pepper and pulse to combine. Set aside until you are ready to cook the lamb.

Make the eggplant puree: Preheat the oven to 400°F (205°C) and line a baking sheet with parchment paper.

Place the eggplant on the prepared baking sheet, pierce the skin a few times with a fork, and roast for about 45 minutes, until it is very soft when pierced with a knife. Remove from the oven and place it on a plate

(recipe continues)

FOR THE LAMB AND ROASTED GARLIC MARINADE:

2 whole racks of lamb, Frenched (have your butcher do this)

2 heads Roasted Garlic (page 16), separated into cloves

1 cup plus 2 tablespoons (255 ml) extra-virgin olive oil

Leaves from 2 sprigs fresh rosemary

Leaves from 2 sprigs fresh thyme

Salt and freshly ground black pepper

FOR THE ROSEMARY-THYME SALT:

3 tablespoons Maldon sea salt

Leaves from 2 sprigs fresh rosemary, minced

Leaves from 4 sprigs fresh thyme, minced

1 teaspoon onion powder

1 teaspoon garlic powder

2 tablespoons freshly ground black pepper

FOR THE EGGPLANT PUREE:

1 medium eggplant (about 1 pound/455 g)

¼ cup (60 ml) heavy cream

Salt and freshly ground white pepper

FOR THE RED WINE DEMI-GLACE:

1 tablespoon extra-virgin olive oil

2 shallots, minced

4 cloves garlic, minced

¼ cup (60 ml) balsamic vinegar

1 sprig fresh rosemary

1 sprig fresh thyme

1½ cups (360 ml) red wine, such as Cabernet or Merlot

1 tablespoon veal demi-glace

1 tablespoon honey

¼ cup (2 ounces/55 g) unsalted butter

Salt and freshly ground black pepper

to cool. Cut the eggplant in half lengthwise, remove the skin from the flesh, and place the flesh in a blender or small food processor.

Pour the cream into a small saucepan and warm it over medium heat for 3 minutes, or until bubbles just start to form. Pour the cream into the blender, season with salt and white pepper, and blend until smooth. Move the eggplant puree to a squeeze bottle and set it aside for plating. Leave the oven on for finishing the lamb.

Make the red wine demi-glace: Heat the oil in a large, heavy-bottomed skillet over medium heat. Add the shallots and cook for 5 minutes, or until translucent, then add the garlic and cook for 2 minutes. Add the vinegar and cook until reduced by about half, 3 to 5 minutes. Stir in the rosemary, thyme, wine, demi-glace, and honey, increase the heat to medium-high, and cook for 10 minutes, or until the sauce has reduced by half. Strain the sauce into a bowl and wipe out the pan. Return the sauce to the pan over low heat and whisk in the butter 1 tablespoon at a time, continuing to whisk until the sauce thickens. Season with salt and pepper.

Cook the lamb: Heat the remaining 2 table-spoons oil in a very large cast-iron skillet over high heat to smoking. Remove the lamb from the marinade and let most of it drip off. Lay the rosemary-thyme salt out on a plate and coat the lamb in the salt on both sides. Place the lamb in the skillet and sear it on each side (but not the ends) for 3 minutes. Transfer the lamb to a baking sheet and roast it to finish for 8 to 10 minutes for medium rare, until an instant-read thermometer inserted diagonally into the center of the meat registers 120°F (50°C). Place the lamb on a cutting board, cover it loosely with aluminum foil, and let it rest for 10 minutes.

To plate: Cut the racks of lamb into four double chops. Squeeze a large circle of eggplant puree onto the middle of each plate, lay two double chops on each plate, and gently drizzle the red wine demi-glace around the eggplant puree. Serve immediately.

The Lees' Favorite Chili

In my career as a DJ, I've had many highs, but many lows as well. It's a tough racket, and to make it in the industry as long as I have, you need amazing people around you. From Tampa to Vegas, my best friend, Ryan Lee, has been that person for the past thirteen years. Ryan now has a beautiful wife, Aida, and is the father of my adorable godson, Marco, and although they love my high-end cooking, their most common requests are my simpler dishes, and this chili is at the top of that list.

SERVES 6
WITH LEFTOVERS FOR CHILI DOGS

Make the chili: In a small food processor or high-speed blender, combine the brown sugar, New Mexico, ancho, guajillo, and árbol chiles and grind them to a powder (it's OK if some larger pieces remain). Set aside.

Heat the oil in a very large saucepan over medium-high heat to almost smoking. Season the sirloin with salt and pepper, add it to the pan, and sear until the juices that release start to dry and the sirloin is browned all over, 7 to 10 minutes. Using a slotted spoon, remove the sirloin to a plate. Add the ground beef, season with salt and pepper, and cook, breaking up the meat with a wooden spoon, until it is cooked through and browned, about 10 minutes. Drain the ground beef through a strainer to remove excess fat, leaving about 2 tablespoons in the pan (or add more to equal 2 tablespoons if your beef was really lean) to cook the onion.

Return the pan to medium-high heat, add half of the ground chiles, and cook, stirring, for 1 minute. Add the onion and cook for 5 minutes, or until lightly colored. Add the roasted garlic, smash it in with the back of a wooden spoon, and cook for 2 minutes. Add the tomato paste and cook for 3 minutes, stirring often. Add the roasted poblano and jalapeño chiles and bell pepper and

FOR THE CHILI:

- ¼ cup (55 g) packed brown sugar
- 2 dried New Mexico chiles, toasted (see page 16), stemmed, seeded, and broken into pieces
- 3 dried ancho chiles, toasted (see page 16), stemmed, seeded, and broken into pieces
- 2 dried guajillo chiles, toasted (see page 16), stemmed, seeded, and broken into pieces
- 1 dried árbol chile, toasted (see page 16), stemmed, seeded, and broken into pieces
- 2 tablespoons extra-virgin olive oil
- 1 pound (455 g) sirloin steak, cut into ¼-inch (6-mm) cubes

Salt and freshly ground black pepper

- 2 pounds (910 g) lean ground beef
- 1 large yellow onion, diced
- 5 cloves Roasted Garlic (page 16)
- 3 tablespoons tomato paste
- 1 poblano chile, roasted (see page 16) and chopped
- 1 jalapeño chile, roasted (see page 16) and chopped
- 1 red bell pepper, roasted (see page 16) and chopped
- 5 chipotle chiles in adobo sauce, finely chopped, with an additional 3 tablespoons of the adobo sauce
- 1 cup (240 ml) beer, preferably Corona
- 1 (28-ounce/785-g) can crushed tomatoes
- 1 (28-ounce/785-g) can diced tomatoes
- 1 cup (240 ml) Chicken Stock (page 20)

FOR THE GARNISHES:

Finely diced yellow onion

Shredded Cheddar cheese

Pickled jalapeño chiles (optional)

Buttered white bread

cook for 3 minutes, stirring often. Add the chipotles and adobo sauce, then add the beer and stir to release any browned bits from the bottom of the pan. Continue to cook until almost all the beer has cooked off, 5 to 7 minutes. Return the sirloin and the ground beef to the pan. Add the crushed tomatoes, diced tomatoes, and stock and bring them to a simmer. Stir in the remaining ground chiles and season heavily with salt and pepper. Reduce the heat to maintain a low simmer, cover, and simmer for 2 hours, stirring occasionally. If you have the time, let the chili sit off the heat, covered, for 30 minutes to further develop its flavor.

To serve: Spoon the chili into bowls and top with diced onion, shredded cheese, and pickled jalapeños, if using. Serve with buttered white bread alongside.

Bourbon-Braised Short Ribs

I love to use bourbon in my cooking as much as I do in my cocktails, as it imparts a natural sweet nuttiness that works so well when braising tough cuts of meat. Braising is by far the best way to prepare short ribs, as the long cooking time and soak in the braising liquid break down their connective tissue to make them melt-in-your-mouth tender. Whenever I make these short ribs, I save half or make extra to use in my Short Rib Ravioli (page 69). I like to serve the short ribs on top of a ring of Roasted Garlic Mashed Potatoes (page 156) or Amaretto–Butternut Squash Puree (page 118).

►►► SERVES 6 ◄◄◄

Make the ribs: Preheat the oven to 300°F (150°C).

Rinse the short ribs under cold water and pat them dry with paper towels. Place them on a plate and allow the short ribs to sit at room temperature for 20 minutes before seasoning. In a small bowl, whisk together the garlic powder, onion powder, and paprika. Season the ribs with salt and pepper and rub them all over with the spice mixture.

Heat the oil in a large Dutch oven or ovenproof saucepan over medium-high heat. Sear the short ribs (working in batches if needed) on all sides until browned all over, about 8 minutes, then transfer the ribs to a plate.

Make the braising liquid: Add 3 tablespoons of the oil to the still-hot Dutch oven over medium-high heat, then add the carrots, celery, onion, leek, roasted garlic, and jalapeño and cook for 10 minutes, or until the vegetables are lightly browned. Add the thyme, parsley, bay leaves, tomato paste, and adobo sauce. Cook, stirring constantly, for about 5 minutes, until the mixture is aromatic

(recipe continues)

FOR THE SHORT RIBS AND RUB:

3½ pounds (1.6 kg) boneless short ribs (about 3 inches/7.5 cm long and at least 1 inch/2.5 cm thick)

1   tablespoon garlic powder

1   tablespoon onion powder

1   tablespoon smoked paprika

Salt and freshly ground black pepper

3   tablespoons extra-virgin olive oil

FOR THE BOURBON BRAISING LIQUID:

5   tablespoons (75 ml) extra-virgin olive oil

2   carrots, finely chopped

2   stalks celery, finely chopped

1   large red onion, finely diced

1   leek, white and light green parts, finely chopped

1   head Roasted Garlic (page 16)

1   jalapeño chile, finely chopped

4   sprigs fresh thyme

8   sprigs fresh flat-leaf parsley

2   bay leaves

2   tablespoons tomato paste

2   tablespoons adobo sauce from canned chipotles

1½ cups (360 ml) bourbon

3   cups (720 ml) Beef Stock (page 20)

Salt and freshly ground black pepper

Garlic Mashed Potatoes (page 156) or Amaretto–Butternut Squash Puree (page 118) and micro arugula, for serving

and the tomato paste and adobo sauce are lightly caramelized and start to stick to the bottom of the pan. Turn the heat off. Pour in the bourbon, stir to release any stuck bits from the bottom of the pan, and cook over medium-high heat for about 3 minutes, until reduced by half. Add the stock and bring it to a boil. Season with salt and pepper. Return the short ribs to the Dutch oven, bring them to a simmer, then turn off the heat and cover. Place in the oven and braise for about 3 hours, until the short ribs are fork-tender.

Transfer the short ribs from the Dutch oven to a wire rack placed over a baking sheet to cool. Strain the braising liquid through a medium-mesh sieve into a large skillet. Cook the liquid over medium-high heat and bring it to a boil. Boil until reduced by half. Transfer the sauce to a squeeze bottle and set it aside for plating.

Finish the short ribs: In a large cast-iron skillet, heat the remaining 2 tablespoons oil over high heat until smoking. Add the short ribs to the skillet and cook on each side for about 2 minutes, until they develop a nice crust on the outside.

To plate: Divide the short ribs among plates, with a scoop of the Roasted Garlic Mashed Potatoes set onto the middle of each plate in a circle. Drizzle with the reduced braising liquid, garnish with micro arugula, and serve.

Dad's Holiday Rib Roast

This recipe is very near and dear to me, as it is the last dish I cooked for my father. I made it for Thanksgiving 2010, and he passed away a week later. However, I do not want this recipe to be mournful, but rather a celebration of my dad, who supported every single crazy, hare-brained idea I ever had. Whether it was music or food, he was always there to back me, and he became a regular guest at my DJ events when he was still healthy enough to show up. Most of my friends have some kind of crazy party story to tell about him. Through the *MasterChef* Finale, I kept a picture of the two of us from when I was young and a few blades of grass from his gravesite in my pocket. I truly believe he was right over my shoulder, cheering me on.

I like to serve this dish with my Crazy Cheese Truffle Mac (page 155), Charred Balsamic Brussels Sprouts (page 152), or Roasted Garlic Mashed Potatoes (page 156). For this recipe, it's worth investing in a probe-style thermometer that stays inside the roast as it cooks; you set a desired internal temp and walk away until it tells you it's ready.

SERVES 4 TO 6

Sear the rib roast: Heat the oil in a large cast-iron skillet over medium-high heat until smoking. Season the roast on all sides very lightly with salt and pepper and sear until nicely browned all over, 2 to 3 minutes per side. Transfer the roast to a baking sheet and let it cool completely.

Make the horseradish crust: In the bowl of a small food processor, combine the horseradish, roasted garlic, rosemary, thyme, salt, pepper, and oil and pulse several

(recipe continues)

FOR THE RIB ROAST:

- 3 tablespoons extra-virgin olive oil
- 1 (5-pound/2.3-kg) bone-in standing rib roast
- Salt and freshly ground black pepper
- 2 carrots, roughly chopped
- 1 red onion, roughly chopped
- 2 stalks celery, roughly chopped
- 1 head garlic, cloves separated but not peeled

FOR THE HORSERADISH CRUST:

- ¾ cup (180 ml) finely grated fresh horseradish (from about 4 ounces/115 g horseradish root)
- 8 cloves Roasted Garlic (page 16)
- Leaves from 2 sprigs fresh rosemary, minced
- Leaves from 4 sprigs fresh thyme, minced
- 6 tablespoons (45 g) Maldon sea salt
- ¼ cup (40 g) freshly ground black pepper
- ½ cup (120 ml) extra-virgin olive oil

FOR THE JUS:

- 1 tablespoon extra-virgin olive oil
- 2 shallots, roughly chopped
- 2 cloves garlic, minced
- ½ cup (120 ml) red wine, such as Cabernet or Merlot
- ½ cup (120 ml) Beef Stock (page 20)
- Salt and freshly ground black pepper

FOR THE HORSERADISH SAUCE:

- ¾ cup (180 ml) sour cream
- ½ cup (120 ml) prepared horseradish
- 1 tablespoon fresh lemon juice
- 1 tablespoon Worcestershire sauce

times to break down the roasted garlic and combine the ingredients. Set it aside until the rib roast has cooled completely.

Cook the rib roast: Cover the roast completely with the horseradish crust, pressing it in so it sticks. Combine the carrots, onion, celery, and garlic in a roasting pan. Place the roast on top of the vegetables fat-cap up. Roast it for about 2½ hours, until an instant-read thermometer inserted through the side of the roast in the deepest part of the meat registers 125°F (52°C) for medium rare. Remove it from the oven to a carving board to rest for 30 minutes, reserving the vegetables and drippings from the pan to make the jus.

Make the jus: While the roast is resting, heat the oil in a small skillet over medium-high heat. Add the shallots and cook for 4 minutes, or until they start to brown, then add the garlic and cook for 1 minute, or until it is aromatic. Add the wine and let it reduce by half, then add the stock and the drippings and vegetables (except the garlic) from the roasting pan and reduce by half once more. Strain the jus into a bowl, then add the garlic and whisk to break it down. Taste and season with salt and pepper if needed.

Make the horseradish sauce: While the jus is reducing, in a medium bowl, whisk together the sour cream, horseradish, lemon juice, and Worcestershire sauce.

To serve: Carve the roast ¼ to ½ inch (6 to 12 mm) thick and serve it with the jus and horseradish sauce on the side.

Honey-Chipotle Hanger Steak

with Roasted Baby Potatoes, Charred Scallions, *and* Chimichurri

This is another very popular recipe around my house, so much so that I used a version of it on *MasterChef* for the Veterans Team Challenge. My team captain, Alejandro, put his faith in me and my dish and our team made my recipe to perfection, leading us to victory. Chef Ramsay, however, was not a fan of the honey-chipotle marinade because of concerns that the sugar in the honey could cause the steak to burn. I stand by this recipe, though, because I absolutely love a little char on my steak. So long as you are paying attention to the pan, you will have no problems. The acid in the chimichurri balances the sweet and spicy marinade for the steak, making this a dish fit for America's bravest!

➡ SERVES 4 TO 6 ◀

Marinate the steak: Place the steaks in a large zip-top bag. In a mini food processor, combine the chipotle, adobo sauce, honey, vinegar, lemon juice, salt, and pepper and pulse to combine the ingredients. Pour the marinade over the steaks and refrigerate to marinate for at least 1 hour and up to overnight.

Make the chimichurri: In the clean bowl of a mini food processor, combine the parsley, cilantro, garlic, jalapeño, and ¼ cup (60 ml) of the vinegar and pulse for about 1 minute to chop and combine, stopping to scrape the sides of the processor as needed. Remove the mixture to a bowl and stir in the remaining ¼ cup (60 ml) vinegar, the sugar, and oil and season with salt and pepper.

(recipe continues)

FOR THE HONEY-CHIPOTLE HANGER STEAK:

- 2 pounds (910 g) hanger steak, cut in half
- 2 tablespoons chipotle chiles in adobo sauce, minced, with an additional 1 teaspoon of the adobo sauce
- 2 tablespoons honey
- 1 teaspoon apple cider vinegar
- Juice of 1 lemon
- 1 teaspoon salt
- ½ teaspoon freshly ground black pepper
- 2 tablespoons extra-virgin olive oil

FOR THE CHIMICHURRI:

- 1 cup (50 g) roughly chopped fresh flat-leaf parsley
- ¼ cup (10 g) roughly chopped fresh cilantro
- 4 cloves garlic, smashed and minced
- ½ jalapeño chile, minced
- ½ cup (120 ml) red wine vinegar
- 1 tablespoon granulated sugar
- 2 tablespoons extra-virgin olive oil
- Salt and freshly ground black pepper

FOR THE ROASTED BABY POTATOES:

- 1 pound (455 g) baby potatoes (about the size of golf balls)
- 3 tablespoons extra-virgin olive oil
- 2 sprigs fresh thyme
- 2 sprigs fresh rosemary
- 5 cloves garlic, smashed
- 2 dried árbol chiles, stemmed and broken into pieces
- Salt and freshly ground black pepper

(ingredients continue)

Make the roasted potatoes: Preheat the oven to 400°F (205°C) and line a roasting pan with parchment paper.

Place the potatoes in a large bowl. Add the oil, thyme, rosemary, garlic, and chiles and season with salt and pepper. Toss to coat the potatoes with the oil and seasonings and transfer them to the prepared roasting pan. Roast for about 30 minutes, until the potatoes are cooked through and browned. Remove the thyme, rosemary, and chiles and place the potatoes in a serving bowl.

Cook the steak: While the potatoes are roasting, remove the steaks from the marinade. Using paper towels, wipe away as much of the marinade as you can and place the steaks on a wire rack set over a baking sheet. Allow them to come to room temperature, 15 to 20 minutes.

Place a large cast-iron skillet over high heat and heat until almost smoking. Add 1 tablespoon of the oil and swirl it around the pan. Season one of the steaks with salt and pepper on both sides. Add the steak to the pan and cook for about 2 minutes on all sides for medium rare. Remove the steak to a clean wire rack placed over a baking sheet. Wipe the pan out, add the remaining 1 tablespoon oil, and cook the second steak the same way you did the first. Let the steaks rest for 7 minutes, then cut them into ½-inch- (12-mm-) thick (or thinner if you prefer) slices against the grain.

Make the charred scallions: While the steaks are resting, add the oil to the skillet you cooked the steak in and heat to smoking. Add the scallions and cook until they are lightly charred, about 5 minutes, flipping them half-way through cooking. Season with salt and pepper.

To plate: Place a small scoop of chimichurri in the middle of each serving plate and divide the hanger steak evenly among the plates. Curl 2 or 3 charred scallions into small bunches and top each plate with a bunch. Finish with some radish microgreens and micro arugula. Serve the roasted potatoes on the side. I like to present them in a small cast-iron pan.

FOR THE CHARRED SCALLIONS:

1 tablespoon extra-virgin olive oil
12 scallions, root ends trimmed
Salt and freshly ground black pepper

FOR THE GARNISHES:

Radish microgreens
Micro arugula

Home Dry-Aged Tomahawk Steak

with Bone Marrow Bordelaise *and* Seared Foie Gras

My favorite combination in the entire food universe is steak and foie gras. Throw some bone marrow in the mix, and this just may be the best representation of my personal tastes on a plate. The steak is the cream of the crop, an insane bone-in tomahawk rib-eye (a very thick-cut rib-eye would make a good substitution). Home dry-aging is simpler than you might think, and the deep meaty flavors that you can achieve from a few days of letting your steak sit in the back of your fridge are nothing less than high-end steakhouse quality. Make sure to use the best-quality meat your butcher offers.

I like to serve this dish with my Au Gratin Potatoes (page 157), Charred Balsamic Brussels Sprouts (page 152), or Roasted Garlic Mashed Potatoes (page 156).

◄ SERVES 4 ►

Dry-age the steak: Wrap the steak tightly in paper towels or cheesecloth and place it on a wire rack over a baking sheet or large plate. Place the steak as far to the back of your fridge as you possibly can. Flip the steak over and change the paper towels every 24 hours over the next 4 days and your steaks are aged. If at any point the paper towel sticks to the steak, peel it off with a knife (any remaining paper towel will come off easily when you salt the steak in the next step).

Cook the steak: Remove the steak from the refrigerator and allow it to come to room temperature, about 30 minutes (since it's a hefty steak, it needs a good

(recipe continues)

FOR THE HOME DRY-AGED TOMAHAWK RIB-EYE:

- 1 (2- to 2½-pound/910-g to 1.2-kg) tomahawk rib-eye steak (or two smaller 2-inch-/5-cm-thick, 1-pound/455-g steaks)
- 1 tablespoon Maldon sea salt

Freshly ground black pepper

- 1 teaspoon garlic powder
- 1 teaspoon onion powder
- 2 tablespoons extra-virgin olive oil
- 3 sprigs fresh rosemary
- 3 sprigs fresh thyme
- 1 head Roasted Garlic (page 16)
- 5 tablespoons Foie Gras Steak Butter (page 18)

FOR THE SEARED FOIE GRAS:

- 8 ounces (225 g) Grade A foie gras

Maldon sea salt and freshly ground black pepper

FOR THE BONE MARROW BORDELAISE:

- 2 tablespoons extra-virgin olive oil
- 2 shallots, roughly chopped
- 5 garlic cloves, smashed and chopped
- ½ cup (120 ml) balsamic vinegar
- 1½ cups (360 ml) red wine, such as Cabernet or Merlot
- 1 cup (240 ml) Beef Stock (page 20)
- 1 (8-inch/20-cm) marrow bone, cut in half lengthwise by your butcher
- 1 sprig fresh rosemary
- 2 sprigs fresh thyme
- 1 tablespoon honey
- ½ stick (2 ounces/55 g) unsalted butter

Salt and freshly ground black pepper

amount of time). Place a large cast-iron skillet in the oven and preheat the oven to 450°F (230°C).

Meanwhile, season the steak all over with the Maldon salt and allow the steak to sit for another 30 minutes to extract even more moisture, massaging the salt in every few minutes (this will help remove any paper that might have stuck to the steak). Season the steak with the pepper, garlic powder, and onion powder. Remove the skillet from the oven and place it over high heat. Add the oil and let it come to smoking. Cook the steak for 4 minutes on each side, or until well browned. You may need to weight the steak with a smaller cast-iron skillet to get the entire sur-face in contact with the skillet. Flip the steak again and add the rosemary, thyme, roasted garlic, and half of the foie gras butter. Let the butter melt, then use a large spoon to baste the steak with the butter for 1 minute, mash-ing the garlic as you do so. Place the skillet in the oven and cook for 5 minutes, then flip the steak, add the remaining foie gras butter, and baste again for 30 seconds. Continue cooking for 3 to 5 minutes, until an instant-read ther-mometer inserted in the center registers 130°F (55°C) for medium rare. Place the steak on a cutting board to rest for about 20 minutes (because of the size of the steak, the resting time is longer than for a standard steak).

Prep the foie gras: While the steak is cooking, place the foie gras in the freezer for 30 min-utes (this makes it easier to slice). Remove the foie gras from the freezer, slice it ¼ inch (6 mm) thick, and score it on one side in a crosshatch pattern with the marks about ¼ inch (6 mm) apart. Place in the refrigerator, then 10 minutes before cooking, move it to the freezer.

Make the bone marrow bordelaise: In a medium, heavy-bottomed skillet, heat the oil over medium-high heat. Add the shallots and cook for about 3 minutes, stirring often, until starting to soften. Add the garlic and cook for another 3 minutes, or until the shallots and garlic are lightly browned. Add the vinegar and reduce by half, 3 to 5 minutes, then add the wine and reduce by half again, about 10 minutes. Pour in the stock, add the marrow bone, rosemary, thyme, and honey, bring them to a boil, and reduce by half one more time, about 10 minutes. Strain the bordelaise into a bowl, reserving the marrow bone, and wipe out the pan. Return the bordelaise to the pan, bring it to a simmer over medium-high heat, and cook for 5 minutes. Remove from the heat and whisk in the butter 1 tablespoon at a time. Season with salt and pepper.

Cook the foie gras: Just before serving, sea-son the foie gras with salt and pepper. Place a nonstick skillet over high heat and heat until extremely hot. If you have an exhaust fan over your stove, now is the time to turn it on, as the foie gras will smoke a lot. Place the foie gras in the skillet scored-side down and cook for 30 seconds to sear it. Flip it and cook for 30 seconds to sear the second side. Remove it to a plate.

To serve: Slice the steak about ¼ inch (6 mm) thick and serve it family style on a large cut-ting board with the marrow bone and the foie gras stacked on the side and the bordelaise in a gravy boat or bowl for pouring.

Mom's Homestyle Flank Steak

There are two dishes I have vivid memories of eating while growing up: my dad's dumplings and my mom's flank steak. The steak is one of those meals that fills the entire house with intense aromas while it's cooking, leading to mouth-watering anticipation! Times and tastes have changed, so my version is quite a bit different from my mom's, with beef stock and Worcestershire sauce adding complexity to the ketchup, and roasted chiles adding a hit of spice. But I did stay true to Mom's cooking method—using a high-sided electric skillet—because I think it is the best tool for the job. That said, you could use a non-electric skillet and cook your steak on the stovetop at the heat levels indicated in the recipe, also with excellent results.

▶ SERVES 4 TO 6 ◀

Score the steak in a crosshatch pattern, making marks about 1 inch (2.5 cm) apart on both sides of the steak.

In a small bowl, whisk together the flour, garlic salt, pepper, paprika, and onion powder. Coat the meat evenly with the flour mixture and set aside.

Combine 1 tablespoon of the oil and the butter in a large, high-sided electric skillet with a lid and heat them to 350°F (175°C) or medium-high, until the butter is melted and bubbling. Add the steak and sear it on each side for 4 minutes, or until nicely browned. Remove the steak to a wire rack placed over a baking sheet.

Add the remaining 1 tablespoon oil and the onion to the skillet and cook for about 5 minutes, stirring often, until they are starting to soften and brown. Add the garlic, celery, and carrots and cook for another 5 minutes. Stir in the bell pepper, jalapeño, and poblano chiles.

(recipe continues)

1½ pounds (680 g) flank steak

2 tablespoons all-purpose flour

2 tablespoons Roasted Garlic Salt (page 17)

1 tablespoon freshly ground black pepper

1 tablespoon smoked paprika

1 teaspoon onion powder

2 tablespoons extra-virgin olive oil

1 tablespoon unsalted butter

1 large yellow onion, diced

4 cloves garlic, minced

2 stalks celery, diced

2 carrots, diced

1 red bell pepper, roasted (see page 16) and diced

1 jalapeño chile, roasted (see page 16) and diced

1 poblano chile, roasted (see page 16) and diced

2½ cups (600 ml) Beef Stock (page 20), plus more if needed

½ cup (120 ml) ketchup

½ cup (120 ml) Worcestershire sauce

6 medium russet potatoes, peeled and cut into 1-inch (2.5-cm) pieces

In a medium bowl, whisk together the stock, ketchup, and Worcestershire sauce. Return the steak to the skillet and pour the stock mixture around the steak. Bring it to a simmer, then cover and reduce the heat to 275°F (135°C) or medium-low and cook for 40 minutes, stirring the vegetables occasionally. If the mixture begins to dry out, add more stock. Add the potatoes and stir them into the sauce. Bring them to a simmer, cover, and cook for 20 to 30 minutes, until the potatoes are cooked through.

Remove the meat from the pan, place it on a cutting board, let it cool slightly, and slice it against the grain. Place the meat in the middle of a large platter, surround it with the vegetables and sauce, and serve it family style.

Ancho and Coffee-Rubbed Venison

with Plum Demi on the Forest Floor

So here it is, my star entree from the *MasterChef* Finale, and the recipe that has become my signature dish! This is one of the most complicated recipes in the entire book, but don't let that intimidate you. If I can do this, so can you! Sure, truffles are not easy to find, and I can't get garlic flowers in any specialty market in Vegas. The idea is to try the recipe with what you can source, and maybe one day while you're strolling through your local farmers' market, you stumble on some garlic flowers or maybe your local specialty food store gets a sample of truffles in, then you can shoot for the stars and go for it.

My goal in creating this dish was to take the judges on a journey into the woods, from the initial look of the plate, to the smell of the smoky plums, and finally to the flavors of a spring morning in the woods with juniper, anise, fiddlehead ferns, and of course those beautiful truffles! When I placed this dish in front of the judges for tasting, Chef Ramsay's reaction was, "Smell that? It smells like the forest." Mission accomplished!

► SERVES 4 ◄

Make the venison rub: In a spice grinder or small food processor, combine the ancho chiles, star anise, allspice, salt, espresso, and sugar and grind them to a powder. Season the venison loins all over with the spice rub and tightly wrap them in plastic wrap to form a long cylinder. Refrigerate them for at least 30 minutes or up to overnight to allow the venison to hold its shape while you proceed with the recipe.

(recipe continues)

FOR THE VENISON AND RUB:

- 2 dried ancho chiles, toasted (page 16), stemmed, seeded, and torn into pieces
- 3 large star anise pods
- 10 allspice berries
- 1½ tablespoons smoked Maldon sea salt or kosher salt
- 2 teaspoons instant espresso powder
- 1½ tablespoons brown sugar
- 2 whole venison tenderloins (about 12 ounces/340 g each)
- 2 tablespoons unsalted butter

FOR THE PLUM DEMI-GLACE:

- 10 juniper berries
- 4 star anise pods
- 1 cinnamon stick
- 1 dried ancho chile, stemmed and seeded
- 2 tablespoons olive oil
- 2 large shallots, roughly chopped
- 6 cloves black garlic (see Notes), peeled
- 1½ cups (360 ml) dry red wine
- 3 plums, halved and chopped
- 1½ cups (360 ml) Beef Stock (page 20)
- 2 tablespoons sherry vinegar

Salt and freshly ground black pepper

FOR THE GARLIC AND SHALLOT CREAM:

- 1 cup (240 ml) whole milk
- 1 cup (240 ml) heavy cream
- 4 large shallots, roughly chopped
- 15 large cloves garlic

Salt and freshly ground white pepper

(ingredients continue)

Make the plum demi-glace: Heat a large skillet over medium heat. Toast the juniper berries, star anise, cinnamon stick, and ancho chile for about 5 minutes, shaking the pan often to avoid burning, until they are fragrant. Remove the spices to a plate and set aside. Pour 1 tablespoon of the oil into the pan, reduce the heat to medium-low, and add the shallots. Cook for about 5 minutes, until they are softened but not colored. Add the black garlic, smash it in with the back of a wooden spoon, and cook for 3 minutes. Return the spices to the pan, add the wine, increase the heat to medium-high, and cook until reduced by about three-quarters, about 10 minutes.

Meanwhile, in a medium saucepan, heat the remaining 1 tablespoon oil over medium heat. Add the plums and cook until some of the juices have been released and the plums are softened, about 10 minutes. Transfer them to a blender and puree until smooth.

Once the wine has reduced, add the stock and cook until reduced by about half, then strain, wipe out the pan, and return the liquid to the pan. Add the plum puree, then add the vinegar and season with salt and pepper. Cook until a spoon leaves a trail behind it when you stir, about 10 minutes. Pour the sauce into a squeeze bottle and set aside while you proceed with the recipe.

Make the garlic and shallot cream: In a medium saucepan, combine the milk and cream over medium heat and bring them to a simmer. Add the shallots and garlic, season with several pinches of salt, reduce the heat to medium-low, and cook for about 30 minutes, until the garlic is very soft. Strain the mixture into a bowl, reserving the liquid, then place the garlic and shallot in a blender and blend until silky smooth, adding 1 teaspoon of the cream mixture at a time through the feed tube if needed to achieve your desired consistency. Season with salt and white pepper. Pour the sauce into a squeeze bottle and set it aside while you proceed with the recipe.

Make the balsamic-glazed cipollini onions: Heat the oil in a medium saucepan over high heat. Add the onions and cook, turning them a few times, until they start to color all over, about 5 minutes, then season them with salt and pepper. Add the vinegar and ¼ cup (60 ml) water,

(recipe continues)

FOR THE BALSAMIC-GLAZED CIPOLLINI ONIONS:

2   tablespoons olive oil

12 cipollini onions, peeled

Salt and freshly ground black pepper

½   cup (120 ml) balsamic vinegar

FOR THE SMOKED PLUMS (SEE NOTE ON EQUIPMENT):

2   plums, halved and thinly sliced

FOR THE PAN-ROASTED CHANTERELLES:

2   tablespoons olive oil

8   ounces (225 g) fresh golden chanterelle mushrooms

2   tablespoons sherry vinegar

2   tablespoons unsalted butter

Salt and freshly ground black pepper

FOR THE ROASTED FIDDLEHEADS:

8   ounces (225 g) fiddlehead ferns, trimmed of any brown stems

2   tablespoons olive oil

2   tablespoons unsalted butter

Salt and freshly ground black pepper

FOR THE GARNISHES:

Shaved black summer truffle (or any truffle for that matter)

Purple garlic flowers

Hearts of fire microgreens or micro basil (they are easier to find than you might think)

reduce the heat to medium-high, and cook, stirring often, until the liquid becomes syrupy and coats the onions, 15 to 20 minutes. Set them aside while you proceed with the recipe.

Smoke the plums: Place the sliced plums in a bowl and, using your smoking gun loaded with cherry wood chips, smoke them for 20 minutes under an airtight cloche.

Cook the venison: Remove the venison from the refrigerator and remove the plastic wrap. Heat a large cast-iron skillet over high heat until lightly smoking. Sear the venison tenderloins on all sides, about 2 minutes on each side. Add the butter to the pan and baste the tenderloins, turning them constantly, for another 3 minutes for medium rare. (I usually add more juniper and anise with the butter while I am basting for an extra flavor boost.) Remove them to a wire rack set over a baking sheet to rest for about 10 minutes while you finish up the recipe.

Make the pan-roasted chanterelles: In large skillet, heat the oil over medium-high heat until lightly smoking. Add the chanterelles and sear until lightly browned, about 6 minutes. Add the vinegar and stir to deglaze the pan. Add the butter and stir to melt it in. Season with salt and pepper, transfer the mushrooms to a bowl, and set aside.

Make the roasted fiddleheads: While the chanterelles are roasting, bring a small pot of water to a boil and salt the water. Add the fiddleheads and blanch them for 20 seconds, then strain. Wipe out the skillet you cooked the chanterelles in, add the oil, and heat over high heat until lightly smoking. Add the fiddleheads and sear until they are deep green in color and tender. Swirl in the butter and season with salt and pepper.

To serve: Place the tenderloins on a cutting board and cut each into six pieces. Squeeze out several quick circles of plum demi sauce in the middle of each serving plate. Place three pieces of venison around the circle, followed by the onions, chanterelles, fiddleheads, and smoked plums, filling in the spaces as you go. Then squeeze small dots of the garlic-shallot cream in and around the plate (different sizes gives a natural feel to the plate). Finish it off with the shaved truffles, garlic flowers, and microgreens and *voila!* You did it!

Notes: Black garlic is a caramelized form of garlic that is made by slowly heating whole bulbs over the course of several weeks. It is very popular in Asian cuisines and can be found in Asian markets and online.

For the smoked plums, I use a battery-powered smoking gun and a glass cloche. These are common items in modernist cooking. The smoking gun is loaded with very fine smoking chips and is lit with a lighter, then a small vacuum sucks the smoke from the bowl and out a tube. The cloche is used to place over whatever you intend to smoke to hold in all the delicious smoky flavor. This is what I did for the *MasterChef* Finale, but if you're not yet ready to take on this modernist technique, the dish will still be award-worthy if you skip it!

SIDES

In the *MasterChef* Kitchen, the perfect side is often elusive.
So much attention is given to perfecting the centerpiece of the
dish that the accompaniments can be overlooked. That is dan-
gerous, as anything that goes on a *MasterChef* plate that's less
than perfect means your time in the competition will be limited.
Team challenges are particularly difficult—with multiple people
and multiple ideas, things can get out of control quickly and side
dishes can quickly spiral downhill.

Many of the recipes in this book come with built-in side
dishes, and the majority of them are interchangeable, in particular
the ones in the meat and poultry chapters. The side dishes in
the following pages are absolute staples in my kitchen and favorites among my friends and family, and it is also safe to say that
this chapter looks a lot like my holiday spread every year. For the
holidays, I don't go crazy with difficult techniques or crazy ingredients. I make what the people around me love, and I love to
make these recipes for them.

Sweet Corn

with Roasted Chiles *and* Queso Fresco

Although I was born in Iowa, I never actually lived there. I was adopted immediately after birth, and my amazing parents moved us to Florida within weeks. My grandparents on my father's side always lived in Iowa, and my father eventually moved back there. What stands out in my memory of Iowa is the miles and miles of cornfields standing tall in the summer. Newfangled corn by-products have reshaped how we eat in this country, and not necessarily in a good way, but the real deal—the stuff straight off the cob—has been with us for a very long time. There are endless ways to prepare fresh corn, but for this recipe I wanted to give it a little Southwestern kick by charring the kernels in a pan, accenting the dish with some sweet roasted peppers, and finishing with a crumble of salty queso fresco.

▶ SERVES 4 TO 6 ◀

Heat a large cast-iron skillet over high heat. Pour in 1 tablespoon of the oil and heat until smoking. Add the corn and sear it until some of the kernels start to blacken, about 5 minutes. Transfer the corn to a plate and set aside.

Pour the remaining 1 tablespoon oil into the pan and lower the heat to medium. Add the onion and cook for 5 minutes, or until translucent. Add the poblano, bell pepper, the roasted and fresh jalapeños, and the garlic and cook for 5 more minutes, or until the fresh

2 tablespoons extra-virgin olive oil

Kernels from 4 ears corn (about 3 cups)

1 medium yellow onion, diced

1 poblano chile, roasted (see page 16) and diced

1 red bell pepper, roasted (see page 16) and diced

2 jalapeño chiles, 1 roasted (see page 16), both diced

2 cloves garlic, minced

½ cup (120 ml) Mexican crema

½ cup (120 ml) whole milk

½ cup (50 g) crumbled queso fresco (see Note)

Salt

jalapeño and garlic are softened. Return the corn to the pan and cook for 3 minutes to combine the flavors. Add the crema and milk and cook until the mixture starts to thicken and resemble creamed corn, about 5 minutes. Remove from the heat, mix in the queso fresco, season with salt, and serve.

Note: Queso fresco is a salty, firm, but crumbly white cheese with a slightly tangy flavor. If you are unable to find it, try substituting feta.

Charred Balsamic Brussels Sprouts

2   thick-cut slices (about ¼ inch/ 6 mm thick) pancetta

1   tablespoon extra-virgin olive oil

12   ounces (340 g) medium Brussels sprouts, ends trimmed, halved

5   ounces (140 g) pearl onions

1½ tablespoons honey

⅓   cup (75 ml) balsamic vinegar

Salt and freshly ground black pepper

For as long as I can remember, I have actually liked Brussels sprouts—maybe I was more of a foodie as a kid than I thought! To get the best flavor out of your Brussels sprouts, you have to give them a good sear, even blacken them in places. Try it and you'll see—you wouldn't believe how many people I have converted to team Brussels sprouts with this recipe!

➡ SERVES 4 TO 6 ⬅

Cut the pancetta into ¼-inch (6-mm) cubes. Heat a large cast-iron skillet over high heat and swirl in the oil. Add the pancetta and cook for 5 minutes, or until it has rendered its fat and starts to get crisp. Using a slotted spoon, transfer the pancetta onto a paper towel–lined plate to drain, leaving the remaining fat in the skillet.

Place the Brussels sprouts cut-side down into the skillet. Spread the onions over the Brussels sprouts. Reduce the heat to medium-high and cook without stirring for about 4 minutes to allow the sprouts to char. Stir with a metal spatula, then cook for an additional 4 to 5 minutes without stirring, until the Brussels sprouts are charred in places, their outer edges begin to soften, and the pearl onions are slightly softened. Return the pancetta to the pan and stir to combine. Stir in the honey and vinegar and cook for about 3 minutes, stirring often, until the honey and vinegar reduce enough to coat the Brussels sprouts with a shiny glaze. Taste and season with salt if needed and some pepper and serve.

Crazy Cheese Truffle Mac

Mac and cheese—America's favorite side dish! The addition of truffle oil takes this to the next level.

━━━► SERVES 4 TO 6 ◄━━━

Make the bread crumb topping: Preheat the oven to 375°F (190°C) and line a baking sheet with parchment paper.

In a large bowl, combine the sourdough cubes, oil, rosemary, and thyme and stir well to coat the cubes in the oil. Season with salt and pepper. Transfer the cubes to the prepared baking sheet and bake for 20 minutes, or until they are crisp. Let them cool, then transfer them to a food processor and process into medium-coarse bread crumbs.

Make the mac and cheese: Bring a large saucepan of salted water to a boil. Add the pasta and cook according to the package instructions for al dente. Drain.

Heat the oil in a large saucepan over medium-high heat. Add the onion and cook for about 5 minutes, stirring often, until lightly colored, then add the garlic and cook for 2 more minutes. Reduce the heat to medium, add the butter, and stir until melted. Add the flour and cook, stirring often, for 5 minutes to form a light roux. Add the three cheeses, milk, and cream, reduce the heat to medium-low, and cook, stirring often, until the cheese is melted and a smooth sauce comes together, about 7 minutes. Stir in the cayenne and truffle oil, then add the pasta and stir to fully coat it in the sauce. Season with salt and pepper. Transfer the mixture to a large cast-iron skillet and cover it with aluminum foil. Bake it for 20 minutes. Remove the foil and cover the mac and cheese with the bread crumbs. Return it to the oven and bake for another 15 to 20 minutes, until the cheese is bubbling and the bread crumbs are golden brown. Serve the mac and cheese family style right out of the skillet.

FOR THE BREAD CRUMB TOPPING:

½   sourdough baguette, cut into 1-inch (2.5-cm) cubes

2   tablespoons extra-virgin olive oil

Leaves from 1 sprig fresh rosemary, finely chopped

Leaves from 2 sprigs fresh thyme, finely chopped

Salt and freshly ground black pepper

FOR THE CRAZY CHEESE TRUFFLE MAC:

Salt

1   pound (455 g) dried Italian cavatappi or penne

2   tablespoons extra-virgin olive oil

1   medium yellow onion, finely diced

3   cloves garlic, minced

5   tablespoons (2½ ounces/70 g) unsalted butter

5   tablespoons (40 g) all-purpose flour

8   ounces (225 g) Gruyère cheese, grated

12 ounces (340 g) white Cheddar cheese, grated

4   ounces (115 g) mozzarella cheese, grated

1   cup (240 ml) whole milk

1   cup (240 ml) heavy cream

1   teaspoon ground cayenne

1½ teaspoons truffle oil

Freshly ground black pepper

Roasted Garlic Mashed Potatoes

5   medium russet potatoes, peeled and cut into 1-inch (2.5-cm) chunks

Salt

2   heads Roasted Garlic (see page 16)

1   stick (4 ounces/115 g) unsalted butter, cut into pieces

¼   cup (60 ml) milk

2   tablespoons grated fresh or prepared horseradish

Freshly ground black pepper

Chopped fresh flat-leaf parsley

Finely chopped fresh chives

My mom can't come to Vegas without getting some of these smooth, creamy, really garlicky mashed potatoes. The roasted garlic elevates a classic American side to a place of elegance and luxury. These potatoes go well with so many dishes and are perfect on a holiday table. Pair them with my Home Dry-Aged Tomahawk Steak (page 137) or Rack of Lamb (page 123) for an over-the-top dinner for friends and family.

SERVES 4 TO 6

Place the potatoes in a large saucepan and add water to cover, then salt the water. Place over high heat and bring to a boil, then reduce the heat to low and cook until the potatoes are fork tender, about 12 minutes. Strain the potatoes into a colander. Press the potatoes through a potato ricer back into the pot (or mash them with a potato masher directly in the pot), adding the roasted garlic intermittently to mix it evenly through the potatoes.

Add the butter, milk, and horseradish and whisk well to melt the butter, combine everything, and smooth out the potatoes. Season with salt and pepper and serve topped with a sprinkle of parsley and chives.

Au Gratin Potatoes

If you've only ever eaten au gratin potatoes from a box, these are a whole new ballgame: creamy, cheesy, and incredibly tender. I love to serve them with my Rack of Lamb (page 123), Herb-Roasted Whole Chicken (page 107), or Home Dry-Aged Tomahawk Steak (page 137).

➤ SERVES 8 ◄

5 tablespoons (2½ ounces/70 g) unsalted butter

1 tablespoon extra-virgin olive oil

1 medium yellow onion, halved and thinly sliced

1 leek, white part only, thinly sliced

4 cloves garlic, minced

2 tablespoons all-purpose flour

4 pounds (1.8 kg) large red potatoes, sliced ⅛ inch (3 mm) thick on a mandoline

1 cup (240 ml) heavy cream

1 cup (240 ml) whole milk

1½ teaspoons salt

1 teaspoon ground cayenne

½ teaspoon freshly grated nutmeg

4 ounces (115 g) Gruyère cheese, grated

4 ounces (115 g) Gouda cheese, grated

Preheat the oven to 375°F (190°C). Grease a 9 by 13-inch (23 by 33-cm) casserole dish with 1 tablespoon of the butter.

In a stockpot, melt the remaining 4 tablespoons (2 ounces/55 g) butter with the oil over medium heat. Add the onion and leek and cook for about 5 minutes, stirring often, until softened. Add the garlic and cook for 1 minute. Add the flour and continue cooking for another 3 to 4 minutes, until the onions, leeks, and garlic are softened and lightly browned. Add the potatoes and stir well, taking care not to break them. Cook for 5 minutes, stirring occasionally, to get them well coated with the flour mixture. Add the cream, milk, salt, cayenne, nutmeg, and half of the cheeses to the pot. Bring them to a simmer and cook, stirring often, for 10 minutes to melt the cheese and coat the potatoes well with the sauce.

Carefully transfer the mixture to the prepared casserole dish and smooth the potatoes into an even layer. Cover tightly with aluminum foil and place it in the oven with a baking sheet underneath to catch any potential drips and bake for 1 hour. Remove the foil and bake for another 15 minutes. Remove from the oven and cover the potatoes with the remaining cheese. Return the pan to the oven and bake until the cheese is melted and bubbly and slightly browned and most of the liquid has been absorbed, about 15 minutes. Remove from the oven and let the potatoes cool for 20 minutes (letting the potatoes sit helps them to hold their shape when you scoop them out of the pan) before slicing and serving.

DESSERTS

When I found out I was going to be on *MasterChef*, I immediately started practicing desserts. I've never considered myself a dessert guy, but after winning two dessert challenges on the show—the Birthday Cake Challenge and the Three Dessert Challenge (milk chocolate cheesecake, white chocolate éclairs, and dark chocolate molten lava cake in one hour!)—that has changed somewhat. The Three Dessert Challenge was by far the most difficult one I have ever seen on *MasterChef*, and somehow I came out on top. The previous twenty-four hours had been the most difficult of the entire season, so when Chef Ramsay cut into that lava cake and I watched it ooze all over the plate, I couldn't hold back my emotions.

I generally cook by feeling and tasting as I go along. In fact, I rarely followed or wrote down a recipe until I sat down to work on this book. I do use science and measurements when playing with molecular gastronomy, but there is a little more wiggle room with flavor there. On the other hand, with baking, measurements must be precise, which made this the most challenging chapter for me to complete. But I'm very happy with the outcome, with recipes including a spin my *MasterChef* Finale dessert, the Salted Caramel–Chocolate Tarts (page 160), and my Candied Bacon Cheesecake (page 163), the first dessert I created that I was really proud of. So strap on your apron, crank up some good tunes, and let's get covered in flour!

Salted Caramel–Chocolate Tarts

with **Berry Sorbet**

Since the airing of the *MasterChef* Finale, the question I've been asked the most is, "Why did you go so simple with your dessert recipe when all season you pushed the limits and took big risks?" The answer is that I wanted to prove that I could show restraint and execute a simple dessert perfectly. To be honest, making a tart isn't really very simple when you have only one hour. Normally, this tart takes about two hours just to set, but by utilizing the blast chiller in the *MasterChef* Kitchen, I was able to successfully pull it off in the time they gave me. Here, I have added a berry sorbet to bring a fresh counterpart to this rich and decadent dessert.

➤ SERVES 6 ◄

Make the sorbet: Heat a medium saucepan over medium heat. Add the oil and berries and cook, stirring occasionally, for 5 minutes, or until the berries start to release their juices. Add the salt and sugar and continue to cook for about 4 minutes, stirring often, until the mixture darkens in color and begins to thicken slightly. Add the wine and cook, stirring often, for 4 minutes, or until the mixture reduces by about one-third. Transfer the mixture to a blender and puree until smooth, then strain the puree through a fine-mesh strainer into a bowl, pressing on the solids to release all the juices. Wipe the saucepan clean and pour the strained berry mixture back into the pan. Place it over high heat and bring to a boil. Remove from the heat and let it cool for 20 minutes, then transfer the mixture to a bowl or container and refrigerate until cold, about 2 hours. Transfer the sorbet base to the bowl of an ice cream maker and churn. Transfer it to a container and freeze the sorbet for at least 4 hours before

(recipe continues)

FOR THE BERRY SORBET:

1 tablespoon extra-virgin olive oil

1¼ pounds (570 g) fresh strawberries, hulled and cut in half

10 ounces (280 g) fresh raspberries

½ teaspoon kosher salt

¼ cup (50 g) granulated sugar

½ cup (120 ml) sweet Riesling wine

Finely grated zest of 1 lemon

Juice of 1 lemon

FOR THE CHOCOLATE-ALMOND PASTRY DOUGH:

1½ cups (190 g) all-purpose flour, plus extra for rolling

¼ cup (30 g) almond flour

¼ cup (25 g) unsweetened cocoa powder

¼ cup (50 g) granulated sugar

¼ teaspoon salt

1 large egg, beaten

1 teaspoon vanilla extract

1 stick (4 ounces/115 g) chilled unsalted butter, cut into ¼-inch (6-mm) cubes, plus more for greasing the pans

2 to 3 tablespoons ice water

FOR THE SALTED CARAMEL:

1½ cups (300 g) granulated sugar

½ teaspoon cream of tartar

½ cup (120 ml) heavy cream

5 tablespoons (2½ ounces/70 g) unsalted butter

2¼ teaspoons fleur de sel

FOR THE CHOCOLATE GANACHE:

6 ounces (170 g) dark chocolate, roughly chopped

¾ cup (180 ml) heavy cream

FOR THE GARNISHES:

Fresh strawberries

Fresh raspberries

Maldon sea salt

using. If you do not have an ice cream maker, transfer the mixture to a freezer-safe bowl and freeze it. Whisk the sorbet vigorously every 20 to 30 minutes for about 4 hours, until a very soft sorbet is formed. Cover the sorbet and let it freeze completely.

Make the pastry dough: In the bowl of a food processor fitted with the blade attachment, combine the all-purpose flour, almond flour, cocoa powder, sugar, and salt and pulse several times to combine. In a small bowl, whisk the egg with the vanilla and set aside. Turn the processor on and add the butter through the feed tube a few cubes at a time, until the mixture breaks down into grainy, pea-size particles. Add the egg mixture through the feed tube, then add the ice water 1 tablespoon at a time, pulsing to combine and checking the consistency of the dough after each addition. Pulse just until the dough begins to hold together in a soft, cohesive ball but is not wet. Shape the dough into a flat disc, wrap it in plastic wrap, and refrigerate for 1 hour before rolling.

Roll the pastry dough: Lightly butter six 4½-inch (11-cm) tart pans and set them onto a baking sheet. Dust a work surface lightly with all-purpose flour and place the dough onto it. Divide the dough into six pieces and roll it out ⅛ inch (3 mm) thick. Brush off excess flour from both sides of the dough. Cut out six 6-inch (15-cm) pastry rounds and carefully press them into the tart pans. Using a rolling pin, press across the top of the tart pans to shear off any excess dough. Refrigerate the tart shells for 1 hour before baking.

Bake the tart shells: Preheat the oven to 350°F (175°C).

Place pie weights or cheesecloth filled with uncooked rice or dried beans in each of the tart pans and blind-bake them for 15 minutes, or until the tarts are firm to the touch. Remove the tart shells from the oven and remove the pie weight. Set the shells aside to cool, then remove them from their pans.

Make the salted caramel: In a medium, high-sided saucepan, combine ½ cup (120 ml) water, the sugar, and cream of tartar and gently stir, taking care not to splash the sides of the pan. Place over medium-high heat and bring them to a boil without stirring. After 5 to 8 minutes, the caramel will slowly change color in spots. When this happens, briefly and gently stir the caramel to encourage even browning. Keep a close watch on the caramel because it can quickly go from ready to burnt. When the caramel begins to turn light golden, reduce the heat to low and cook until it turns deep golden brown. Immediately remove the pan from the heat and slowly add the cream a little at a time, whisking continuously. The mixture will bubble and rise up, so pay close attention and only add more cream as the hot caramel settles down in the pan. When all the cream has been added, whisk in the butter 1 tablespoon at a time until it is incorporated, then whisk in the fleur de sel. Carefully fill each of the tart shells with about ⅛ inch (3 mm) of the hot caramel and set them aside to cool.

Make the chocolate ganache: In a bowl placed over a pan filled with a couple inches of water (make sure the water doesn't touch the bowl), combine the chocolate and cream. Bring the water to a simmer over low heat and stir the chocolate and cream with a heatproof spatula until the chocolate is fully melted and the mixture is homogeneous. Pour the ganache on top of the cooled caramel, filling the tart shells to the top. Refrigerate the tarts to set up the ganache and cool completely, about 30 minutes.

To serve: Place a tart on a serving plate and top with a quenelle of the berry sorbet and some fresh strawberries and raspberries. Sprinkle with a pinch of Maldon salt. Repeat with the remaining tarts and serve.

Candied Bacon Cheesecake

with **Blackberry Coulis**

My friend Ryan bought me a bottle of bacon-flavored soda as a gag Christmas present a few years back, and it got me playing around with unexpected bacon combinations. Candied bacon was the highlight of my bacon experimentation, and working it into cheesecake turned out to be a pairing made in dessert heaven. You might want to make a double batch of the candied bacon, because if you're like me, you'll find yourself eating half of it before you get to the cheesecake.

➤ SERVES 4 ◄

Make the candied bacon: Preheat the oven to 400°F (205°C).

Pour the bourbon into a medium saucepan and bring it to a boil over high heat. Reduce the heat to medium-high and simmer for about 10 minutes, until reduced to ¼ cup (60 ml). Add ½ cup (110 g) of the brown sugar, the salt, and red pepper flakes and stir until the sugar dissolves. Remove from the heat and let it cool for about 5 minutes. Arrange the bacon in a single layer on a wire rack set over a parchment-lined baking sheet. Using a pastry brush, brush the bourbon mixture over the bacon and sprinkle it with half of the remaining brown sugar. Flip the bacon over onto the rack and repeat with the remaining bourbon mixture and brown sugar. Bake the bacon on the rack for about 20 minutes, until crisp and well browned. The bacon slices on the edge of the baking sheet may cook faster, so you may need to remove those pieces before the others. The bacon will appear darker than plain cooked bacon; this is OK.

(recipe continues)

FOR THE CANDIED BACON:

1   cup (240 ml) bourbon

1   cup (220 g) packed brown sugar

1   teaspoon salt

1   teaspoon red pepper flakes

1   pound (455 g) maple bacon

FOR THE CHEESECAKE:

2   tablespoons butter, softened, for the pans, plus ⅓ cup (2½ ounces/ 70 g) unsalted butter, melted

1½ cups (180 g) finely ground graham cracker crumbs (from about 1 sleeve of crackers)

12 ounces (340 g) cream cheese, at room temperature

½   cup (100 g) granulated sugar

2   large eggs

1   teaspoon vanilla extract

½   cup (120 ml) sour cream

FOR THE BLACKBERRY COULIS:

1   tablespoon extra-virgin olive oil

6   ounces (170 g) fresh blackberries

¼   cup (50 g) granulated sugar

1   teaspoon finely grated lemon zest

2   tablespoons fresh lemon juice

Pinch of salt

Reduce the oven temperature to 325°F (165°C). Allow the bacon to cool completely, then set aside four slices for garnish. Crumble the remaining bacon, place it in a food processor fitted with a blade attachment, and grind it into small, lentil-size pieces.

Make the cheesecake: Coat the bottom of four 4½-inch (11-cm) springform pans with the 2 tablespoons butter. In a medium bowl, combine the ⅓ cup (2½ ounces/70 g) melted butter and the graham cracker crumbs and mix well. Divide the graham cracker mixture among the pans and press it evenly onto the bottom of the pans, using the bottom surface of a measuring cup to smooth the crumbs flat. Bake the crusts for about 10 minutes, until firm and lightly browned. Place them on cooling racks to cool completely.

Line a large, deep baking dish with a double layer of heavy-duty aluminum foil (this will help prevent water from seeping into the cheesecakes). Bring a kettle or large pot of water to a simmer for the water bath.

In the bowl of a stand mixer fitted with the paddle attachment, combine the cream cheese and granulated sugar and beat at medium speed until incorporated, scraping down the sides of the bowl with a rubber spatula as needed. Add the eggs one at a time, beating for 1 minute after each addition, until fully incorporated. Add the vanilla and beat for 30 seconds. Remove the bowl from the mixer and, using a rubber spatula, fold in the sour cream and ¼ cup (55 g) of the ground candied bacon until the cream cheese is fully incorporated and there are no white specks remaining. Divide the batter among the pans and lightly jiggle them to evenly distribute the batter. Place the cheesecakes into

the foil-lined pan and turn the foil upward to create a wall around the pans. Pour the hot water into the baking dish outside of the foil wrap to reach halfway up the sides of the pans. Bake for 25 minutes, or until the center of the cheesecakes no longer jiggle. Remove the pan from the oven, place the cheesecakes on cooling racks, and let them cool completely. Then cover with plastic wrap and refrigerate until completely set, about 2 hours. Remove each cheesecake from the pan by running a flat metal spatula around the inside edge and unclipping the ring.

Make the blackberry coulis: In a medium saucepan, combine the oil and blackberries. Place them over medium-high heat and cook for about 5 minutes, until the berries release their juices. Transfer them to a blender and puree until smooth. Return the mixture to the saucepan, add the granulated sugar, place the pan over medium-high heat, and cook for 3 minutes, stirring often, or until the mixture slightly thickens and has a syrupy consistency. Add ½ cup (120 ml) water, the lemon zest, lemon juice, and salt and cook for about 3 minutes, until the mixture is thick and syrupy and coats the back of a spoon. Strain the coulis through a fine-mesh strainer into a bowl, pressing on the solids to extract all of the liquid. Set the coulis aside to cool.

To serve: Place one mini cheesecake in the center of a large white plate, top with blackberry coulis, and cover the entire top with some of the remaining ground candied bacon. Lean a slice of reserved candied bacon against the side of the cake. Repeat with the remaining cheesecakes.

Perfect Lemon Meringue Pie

Early on in the *MasterChef* Kitchen, we faced our first baking challenge: pie! I will admit I was quite nervous going into it, so I went with an American classic that requires minimal baking. To my surprise, my pie was one of the top three of the night. I have tweaked the recipe here based on some of the feedback the judges gave me. Chef Ramsay's critique was that my meringue could have been a little stiffer and higher on the pie and Chef Aaron Sanchez would have liked a little more lemon curd. Problems now solved! As you might imagine, this challenge had me the most intimidated by Chef Christina Tosi, but, to my relief, she really liked my pie.

SERVES 6 TO 8

Make the pie crust: In the bowl of a food processor fitted with the blade, pulse the flour and salt to combine. Add the butter and pulse until the mixture resembles wet sand. In a small bowl, whisk together the egg, cream, and water. With the processor running, slowly add the egg mixture through the feed tube until the dough forms a loose ball.

Flour a work surface, then remove the dough to the work surface and quickly form it into a disc (this should take no longer than 1 minute; any longer, and you run the risk of overdeveloping the gluten). Wrap the dough in plastic wrap and freeze it for 20 minutes.

Grease a 9-inch (23-cm) pie pan. Remove the dough from the freezer and place it on a floured work surface. Cut the dough in half, wrap one half well in plastic wrap, and freeze it for another pie. Roll out the remaining dough into a large circle roughly ⅛ inch (3 mm) thick by 11 inches (28 cm) in diameter. Fit the dough into the prepared pie pan (there should be

(recipe continues)

FOR THE PIE CRUST:

- 2½ cups (315 g) all-purpose flour, plus extra for rolling
- 1 teaspoon salt
- 1½ sticks (6 ounces/170 g) cold unsalted butter, cut into ½-inch (12-mm) cubes
- 1 large egg
- 3 tablespoons heavy cream
- ¼ cup (60 ml) ice water
- 1 large egg white

FOR THE LEMON CURD:

- 1 cup (200 g) granulated sugar
- 1½ teaspoons grated lemon zest
- 3 tablespoons cornstarch
- 2 tablespoons all-purpose flour
- ¼ teaspoon salt
- ½ cup (120 ml) fresh lemon juice
- 2 tablespoons unsalted butter, softened
- 4 large egg yolks

FOR THE MERINGUE:

- 4 large egg whites
- ⅛ teaspoon cream of tartar
- 6 tablespoons (75 g) granulated sugar

about a ½-inch/12-mm overhang). Trim off any excess dough and tuck the overhang under itself on the rim of the pan, building up the rim of crust. Crimp or flute the rim of your pie. Refrigerate the pie crust for 1 hour before baking.

Preheat the oven to 375°F (190°C).

In a small bowl, whisk together the egg white and 2 tablespoons water and brush the egg wash over the edges of the pie (do not brush it on the bottom or your pie weights may stick). Place pie weights or cheesecloth filled with dry beans in the bottom of the pie and blind-bake it for about 20 minutes, removing the weights during the last 5 minutes, until the crust is golden brown all over. Set the crust onto a cooling rack to cool.

Make the lemon curd: Place the sugar in a small bowl, add the lemon zest, and use your fingers to rub it in to release some of its essential oils. In a medium saucepan, whisk together the sugar mixture, cornstarch, flour, salt, lemon juice, and 1¾ cups (420 ml) water. Place it over medium-high heat and cook, stirring continuously, until the mixture comes to a boil and thickens enough to coat the back of a spoon, 7 to 10 minutes. Whisk in the butter.

In a medium bowl, whisk the egg yolks until combined, then take ¼ cup (60 ml) of the cooked sugar mixture and slowly pour a small steady stream into the egg yolks, whisking continuously to temper the yolks. Pour the tempered egg yolk mixture back into the saucepan, whisking continuously, and continue cooking for about 3 minutes, whisking constantly, until the lemon curd thickens considerably and thickly coats the back of a spoon. Pour the hot lemon curd into the baked pie crust and shake it lightly to evenly spread out the mixture. Refrigerate the pie to cool it.

Make the meringue: Place the egg whites in the bowl of a stand mixer fitted with the whisk attachment and beat them on medium-low speed until lightly frothy and bubbly. Add the cream of tartar, increase the speed to medium-high, and continue beating until the egg whites begin to turn white. Add the sugar and beat until the whites hold stiff peaks, 4 to 6 minutes. Do not overbeat, or the meringue will break and become grainy. Scoop the meringue onto the cooled lemon curd and spread it out evenly. Using a rubber spatula, gently dip in and out of the meringue to create lots of peaks across the pie. Toast the meringue with a culinary torch (or place it under the preheated broiler) for 30 seconds to lightly brown the meringue. Serve immediately or store, loosely covered with foil, in the refrigerator for up to 3 days.

Brandi Mudd's Country Madeleines

One of the most amazing parts of the *MasterChef* experience was the amazing friendships I made along the way. Brandi Mudd and I hit it off on the very first day over a turkey sandwich. It takes something special like *MasterChef* to create a tight friendship between a fifth-grade schoolteacher from Kentucky and a nightclub DJ from Las Vegas. From that first meeting, I knew she would be a tough competitor, and I actually predicted she and I would be in the *MasterChef* Finale together.

I asked Brandi to recreate her madeleine recipe from the *MasterChef* Finale for my book because I was blown away with the beauty of her finished plate. When you're from the South, rich ingredients such as caramel and bourbon are a must! But even we Southerners at times enjoy a light and airy dessert, and this recipe deliciously embraces both. Although this is a composed dessert, the madeleines are amazing on their own, so if you don't have time to complete the entire recipe, just shoot for the madeleines.

SERVES 8
MAKES ABOUT 24 MADELEINES

Make the madeleine batter: In a medium bowl, whisk together the all-purpose flour, P.A.N. cornmeal, yellow cornmeal, baking powder, and salt. In a stand mixer fitted with the whisk attachment, combine the eggs and granulated sugar and whisk on medium-high speed for about 2 minutes, until the mixture is pale and thick. Whisk in the honey to incorporate it. Remove the bowl from the mixer and, using a rubber spatula, fold in the flour mixture. Pour the melted butter in a slow, steady

(recipe continues)

FOR THE MADELEINES:

- 1 cup (125 g) all-purpose flour, plus more for the pans
- ¼ cup (40 g) P.A.N. cornmeal (see Note)
- ¼ cup (45 g) fine yellow cornmeal
- 1 teaspoon baking powder
- ½ teaspoon salt
- 4 large eggs
- ⅔ cup (135 g) granulated sugar
- 2 tablespoons honey
- 1½ sticks (6 ounces/170 g) unsalted butter, melted, plus 2 tablespoons for the pan

Confectioners' sugar for dusting

FOR THE WHITE CHOCOLATE MOUSSE:

- 1 (¼-ounce/10-g) envelope powdered gelatin
- 12 ounces (340 g) white chocolate, roughly chopped
- 2½ cups (600 ml) heavy cream

Pinch of salt

FOR THE CARAMELIZED PECANS:

- 1 large egg white
- ½ cup (50 g) pecan halves
- ¼ cup (55 g) packed brown sugar

FOR THE CARAMEL SAUCE:

- 1 cup (200 g) granulated sugar
- ¾ stick (3 ounces/85 g) unsalted butter
- ½ cup (120 ml) heavy cream
- ¼ cup (60 ml) bourbon

Pinch of salt

(ingredients continue)

stream down the inside edge of the bowl, folding the batter gently to combine. Cover the bowl with plastic wrap and refrigerate it for at least 4 hours or overnight.

Make the white chocolate mousse: In a small bowl, dissolve the gelatin in ¼ cup (60 ml) warm water and set it aside for 5 minutes. Fill a large bowl with ice and water to make an ice water bath and rest a thin metal bowl on top of the water. Place the white chocolate in a bowl placed over a pan filled with a couple inches of water (make sure the water doesn't touch the bowl). Bring the water to a simmer over low heat and stir with a heatproof spatula until the white chocolate is melted. In a small saucepan, heat ¾ cup (180 ml) of the cream over medium-high heat until it comes to a boil, then whisk in the gelatin and continue to whisk for 30 seconds, or until the gelatin is dissolved. Slowly add the cream to the melted chocolate, whisking continuously until incorporated. Place the chocolate-cream mixture over the ice bath and continue to whisk until the mixture cools to room temperature. Add the salt and whisk to combine.

Pour the remaining 1¾ cups (420 ml) of the cream into the bowl of a stand mixer fitted with the whisk attachment and whip it on high speed until the cream barely holds stiff peaks. Gently fold the whipped cream into the chocolate mixture a small amount at a time. Fold with a light hand so the mousse retains a light, airy texture. Cover the bowl with plastic wrap and refrigerate the mousse for at least 1 hour or up to 2 hours to set up. The mousse can be lightly whisked to soften it for plating if needed, and if you have any left over at the end, enjoy a bowlful on its own (it will keep for a couple days in the refrigerator).

Bake the madeleines: Preheat oven to 400°F (205°C) and butter and flour the madeleine pans.

Using a spoon or pastry bag, fill each madeleine mold about three-quarters full. Bake until the madeleines are golden around the edges and the tops are firm to touch, 15 to 20 minutes, depending on the size and thickness of the pan. Remove the pans from the oven and immediately release the madeleines from their molds by rapping them against a cooling rack. Dust them with confectioners' sugar.

FOR THE PEACH SLURRY:

2 large ripe peaches

2 tablespoons granulated sugar

1 tablespoon cornstarch

FOR THE PEACHES FLAMBÉ:

4 large ripe peaches

2 tablespoons unsalted butter

3 tablespoons brown sugar

Pinch of salt

3 tablespoons bourbon

FOR THE GARNISH:

Assorted small edible flowers

Make the pecans: Reduce the oven temperature to 350°F (175°C) and line a baking sheet with parchment paper. Whisk the egg white in a small bowl to break it up. Add the pecans and brown sugar and mix until the ingredients are well blended. Spread the mixture onto the baking sheet in a single layer and bake until the sugar is caramelized and the nuts are well browned, 8 to 10 minutes. Keep a close eye on them so they don't burn. Remove the nuts to a cooling rack to cool completely, then roughly chop them and set them aside for garnish.

Make the caramel sauce: Place the granulated sugar in a medium saucepan, pour ¼ cup (60 ml) water over the top, and stir carefully to incorporate the ingredients. Cook over medium heat for 8 to 10 minutes without stirring. The caramel will begin to bubble and slowly change color. Keep a close watch on it, because it can quickly go from ready to burnt. When the caramel turns a deep amber brown, immediately remove the pan from the heat. Add the butter and whisk to combine, then add the cream in four additions, stirring continuously. The mixture will bubble and rise up, so pay attention and only add more cream after the caramel settles down in the pan. Whisk in the bourbon and salt and transfer to a bowl.

Make the peach slurry: Using a vegetable peeler, peel the peaches and slice them. Place them in a food processor, add 2 tablespoons water, and process until smooth. Place the peach puree in a medium saucepan, add the granulated sugar, place the pan over medium heat, and bring it to a simmer. Remove 2 tablespoons of the peach puree to a small bowl, add the cornstarch, and whisk until dissolved. Return the cornstarch mixture to the pan and simmer until the mixture thickens enough to coat the back of a spoon, about 4 minutes. Place the peach slurry in the refrigerator until cooled and thin it with a bit of water if necessary.

Make the peaches flambé: Using a vegetable peeler, peel and slice each peach into twelve wedges that are about ½ inch (12 mm) thick. Heat the butter in a large cast-iron skillet over high heat. When the butter is melted and sizzling, add the peaches and sprinkle on the brown sugar and salt. Cook, stirring with a metal spatula, until the sugar dissolves and the peaches are beginning to soften but still hold their shape, about 3 minutes. Hold the pan at a diagonal over the open flame of the burner and pour the bourbon into the pan. Set the bourbon aflame with a stick lighter, allow the flames to cook off and die down, then cook, stirring, for 2 to 3 minutes, until the liquid is reduced and caramelized and the peaches are lightly browned. (If you don't have a stick lighter, simply cook until the bourbon reduces down.) Transfer the peaches from the pan onto a plate and set aside.

To plate: On a large white plate, use a pastry brush to paint a thick 3-inch (7.5-cm) strip of caramel sauce down the left side of the plate, leaving about 2 inches (5 cm) from the edge of the plate clear. Set three mounds of mousse (about 1½ inches/4 cm in diameter) in a zigzag down the caramel sauce strip. Rest a madeleine against each mousse mound and carefully arrange four peach slices around the madeleines, working down the caramel strip. Make five small (about ½ inch/12 mm in diameter) dots of mousse on the caramel strip from one end of the plate to the other and sprinkle some pecans on top of the mousse dots. Pour the peach slurry loosely down the caramel strip and set a few edible flowers around the plate. The entire right side of the plate is left completely empty.

Note: P.A.N. is a brand of precooked cornmeal used heavily in South American countries. It is finer than regular cornmeal, resulting in a much airier final product. You can find it in Latin American markets.

Dark Chocolate Soufflés

with Orange Cream *and* Strawberry Drizzle

When done perfectly, soufflés are the lightest, fluffiest, most delicate dessert imaginable, but when things go wrong, it can be a disaster in your oven! Trust me, I have had my fair share of soufflé eruptions, and they are not at all fun to clean up. A recent dinner at a legendary New York City steakhouse ended with an amazing Grand Marnier soufflé that inspired this modernist spin featuring an orange cream charged in a whipping siphon. It's a great technique for any of you just getting your feet wet with modernist cooking, but if you're not quite up for it, there's an option for whipping your cream the good old-fashioned way, with an electric mixer.

⬛➡ SERVES 8 ⬅⬛

Make the orange cream: In a small bowl, combine the cream and orange zest, cover with plastic wrap, and refrigerate them to infuse for at least 30 minutes or overnight.

Strain the cream into a medium bowl and whisk in the confectioners' sugar. Now jump down to the end of the recipe to read the Note about working with whipping siphons. Once you've got the cautions down, add the cream to your whipping siphon, fit it with two chargers, shake well, and refrigerate it for at least 15 minutes or up to 1 hour. Shake again and test. You may have to release some of the gas by lightly pulling on the trigger; make sure you cover the nozzle with a towel when you do this. If you don't have a whipping siphon, pour the cream mixture into the bowl of a stand mixer fitted with the whisk attachment and whip on medium speed until the

(recipe continues)

FOR THE ORANGE CREAM (SEE NOTE FOR SPECIAL EQUIPMENT):

1 cup (240 ml) heavy cream

Zest of 2 oranges

½ cup (65 g) confectioners' sugar

FOR THE STRAWBERRY DRIZZLE:

12 ounces (340 g) fresh strawberries, hulled and cut in half

½ cup (100 g) granulated sugar

¼ cup (60 ml) champagne vinegar or white balsamic vinegar

Juice of ½ lemon

Pinch of salt

FOR THE CHOCOLATE SOUFFLÉS:

4 teaspoons unsalted butter, at room temperature

1 cup plus 2 tablespoons (225 g) granulated sugar

3 ounces (85 g) dark chocolate, roughly chopped

2 cups (190 g) unsweetened cocoa powder

2 teaspoons vanilla extract

5 large egg whites, at room temperature

Pinch of salt

cream thickens to medium stiff peaks, taking care not to overwhip.

Make the strawberry drizzle: Place the strawberries in a medium saucepan over medium heat and cook until they release their juices, about 8 minutes. Add the granulated sugar and cook, stirring, for 5 minutes, or until slightly syrupy. Add ¼ cup (60 ml) water, the vinegar, lemon juice, and salt and cook until the mixture darkens in color and thickly coats the back of a spoon, about 10 minutes. Transfer the mixture to a blender and puree until smooth, adding more water 1 tablespoon at a time if needed to thin out the sauce to a smooth, thick, syrupy consistency. Strain the sauce through a fine-mesh strainer into a bowl, pressing on the solids to release all the liquid. Transfer the puree to a squeeze bottle for plating.

Make the chocolate soufflés: Lightly butter eight 6-ounce (170-g) ramekins and coat them with 2 tablespoons of the sugar. Run your finger along the top ¼ inch (6 mm) of the rim to wipe off the butter and sugar (this will help the soufflés attach to the ramekins and rise). Place the ramekins on a parchment-lined baking sheet.

Preheat the oven to 350°F (175°C) and set an oven rack to the middle position.

Place the chocolate in a bowl placed over a pan filled with a couple inches of water (make sure the water doesn't touch the bowl). Bring the water to a simmer over low heat and stir the chocolate with a heatproof spatula until it is melted.

In a medium saucepan, bring 2¾ cups (660 ml) water to a simmer and whisk in half of the cocoa powder. Increase the heat to medium-high and whisk constantly until the cocoa powder and water are homogeneous. Add the remaining cocoa powder and whisk until the mixture is smooth and creamy. Add the melted chocolate and vanilla and whisk to incorporate, then cook for 1 minute, or until slightly thickened. Remove from the heat and, using a rubber spatula, scrape the chocolate mixture into a large bowl.

Combine the egg whites and salt in the bowl of a stand mixer fitted with the whisk attachment. Whisk on medium speed until the whites become frothy, then increase the speed to medium-high and add one quarter of the remaining 1 cup (200 g) sugar. As the whites begin to increase in volume, increase the speed to high, add the remaining sugar in a steady stream, and whip until the whites hold medium-stiff peaks.

Using a large rubber spatula, fold about one third of the whites into the warm chocolate mixture. Add the remaining whites and gently fold them in until there are no remaining visible streaks or bubbles of white meringue.

Carefully scoop the batter into the ramekins, filling them to within ¼ inch (6 mm) of the top. Bake for 18 to 20 minutes, until they no longer jiggle, the tops have risen about 1 inch (2.5 cm) above the rim, and a crust forms on the top. Be careful to not overbake or the soufflés will dry out. Remove the soufflés from the oven.

To plate: As you take the soufflés out of the oven, generously cover the tops with strawberry drizzle so it cascades down the sides. Top with a generous squeeze or dollop of orange cream and serve immediately.

Note: For the modernist whipped cream, you'll need two N_2O whipped cream chargers and a whipping siphon. You can find these in kitchen stores and online. When working with whipping siphons, never fill the canister beyond the maximum filling amount (there is a line marked on the outside of most canisters). Don't use fruit with pulp or seeds and never insert the charger if the decorating tip isn't attached to the dispensing valve. Do not unscrew the device head from a pressurized device.

White Chocolate Panna Cotta

with Raspberry Coulis

FOR THE WHITE CHOCOLATE PANNA COTTA:

1   cup plus 2 tablespoons (255 ml) whole milk

1½ teaspoons powdered gelatin

1   cup (240 ml) heavy cream

1½ tablespoons granulated sugar

3   ounces (85 g) white chocolate, finely chopped

Pinch of salt

FOR THE RASPBERRY COULIS:

¼ cup (50 g) granulated sugar

12 ounces (340 g) fresh raspberries

2   tablespoons fresh lemon juice

FOR THE GARNISHES:

2   ounces (55 g) white chocolate

Fresh raspberries

Small fresh mint leaves

If you watched *MasterChef*, you know I have a deep love for all things Italian. From food to history and culture, I can't get enough of Italy! *Panna cotta* is Italian for "cooked cream," and that is exactly what it is—sweetened cream thickened with gelatin and set in some type of a mold. Panna cotta is a silky, smooth, luxurious dessert that is surprisingly simple to prepare. The hardest part about making panna cotta is waiting for it to set so you can devour it! The white chocolate brings an incredible depth to my take on panna cotta, and raspberries brighten it up with a fresh burst of berry flavor.

SERVES 4 TO 6

Make the panna cotta: Pour 2 tablespoons of the milk into a small bowl, sprinkle the gelatin over the top, and set it aside for 5 to 10 minutes to allow the gelatin to bloom.

Meanwhile, in a medium, heavy-bottomed saucepan, whisk together the cream, the remaining 1 cup (240 ml) milk, and the sugar. Place them over medium-high heat and bring them just to a boil. Remove from the heat and whisk in the white chocolate and the bloomed gelatin until they are thoroughly incorporated, smooth, and homogenous. Whisk in the salt and pour the mixture into four to six serving glasses. A nice choice would be wine glasses without stems so you can see the layers. Cover and refrigerate them for about 3 hours to set.

Make the raspberry coulis: In a medium saucepan, whisk together the sugar and ¼ cup (60 ml) water. Place the pan over medium-high heat and whisk until the sugar has dissolved, about 1 minute. Add the raspberries, reduce the heat to medium, and cook for 8 to 10 minutes, stirring often, until the mixture begins to thicken slightly and releases syrupy juices. Add the lemon juice and cook for about 2 minutes, until the mixture coats the back of a spoon. Transfer the berry mixture to a blender and puree until smooth. Pour the coulis through a fine-mesh strainer into a bowl and let it cool for 5 minutes. Pour the coulis evenly over the tops of the cooled panna cotta, then return them to the refrigerator for 1 hour to set.

To serve: Remove the panna cottas from the refrigerator. Using a Microplane, grate the white chocolate over the top of each panna cotta, top with three raspberries per glass, and finish with a few mint leaves.

COCKTAILS & SNACKS

Here it is, the booze and bar food chapter! How many of you jumped straight to this page? If you did, I agree with your decision. I always enjoy a good cocktail while I'm busy at work in the kitchen. I love to cook with bourbon, and I love to drink it as well, so many of my cocktails are bourbon based. And the snacks cover all the tastes—salty, sweet, spicy, and tart—that I crave when I'm out for cocktails with friends.

Vegas is a leader in the craft cocktail explosion. The bartenders here are pushing the limits of creativity, so I took the time to make sure my city would approve of these cocktails by consulting on the recipes with my best friends and two of the city's top bartenders, Ryan Lee and Chuck Englehardt. Fresh herbs, dried chiles, and citrus play large roles in my cocktails: For example, thyme, basil, and dried chiles work exceptionally well with bourbon, and the Burnt Blue Rosemary Gin Smash (page 192) gives you an unexpected hint of rosemary. Make sure to have a big batch of my Spicy Garlic Chicken Wings (page 186) and Baked Brie with Bourbon-Pecan-Maple Drizzle (page 180) on hand for your next cocktail party to go with these amazing drinks!

Baked Brie

with Bourbon-Pecan-Maple Drizzle

For this chapter, I wanted to do more than just give you an outline for a great cheese tray to go with your cocktails. Try this spin on the cheese course at your next cocktail party and you'll blow your guests away.

━━━━▶ SERVES 6 TO 8 ◀━━━━

Make the sourdough toasts: Preheat the oven to 375°F (190°C) and line two baking sheets with parchment paper.

Place the sourdough slices on one of the prepared baking sheets. Using a pastry brush, brush the top of each slice with oil. Bake for 10 to 15 minutes, until slightly crisp and lightly browned around the edges. Remove from the oven and place the pan on a wire rack or plate until ready to serve.

Bake the Brie: Set the Brie onto the second prepared baking sheet (or into an oven-safe dish) and bake it for about 20 minutes, until the cheese is very soft and begins to ooze out.

Make the bourbon-pecan-maple drizzle: Pour the bourbon into a small saucepan and bring it to a boil over high heat. Reduce the heat to medium-high and boil for about 5 minutes, until the bourbon is reduced by about three quarters. Add the honey, maple syrup, and lemon juice and stir to combine. Return the mixture to a boil and boil for 6 to 8 minutes, until the mixture is a deep amber color and reduces by about one third. Remove the pan from the heat, stir in the pecans and cranberries, and season lightly with salt.

To serve: Remove the Brie from the oven and place it on a serving platter. Pour the bourbon-pecan-maple drizzle over the Brie, arrange the sourdough toasts around the outside rim of the cheese platter, and serve.

1   sourdough baguette (about 14 ounces/400 g), cut into ¼-inch (6-mm) slices

¼   cup (60 ml) extra-virgin olive oil

1   (1-pound/455-g) wheel Brie cheese

¾   cup (180 ml) bourbon

¼   cup (60 ml) honey

¼   cup (60 ml) maple syrup

1   tablespoon fresh lemon juice

¼   cup (25 g) pecans, chopped

¼   cup (35 g) dried cranberries

Salt

Pickled Cantaloupe, page 184, *and* Pickled Cukes, opposite

Pickled Cukes

2 tablespoons pickling spice

5 dried árbol chiles

¾ cup (180 ml) distilled white vinegar

¾ cup (180 ml) white wine vinegar

¼ cup (50 g) granulated sugar

2 tablespoons kosher salt

6 Kirby or pickling cucumbers, quartered lengthwise

4 sprigs fresh dill

3 cloves garlic, peeled

I always have a mason jar of homemade pickles of some sort in my fridge—I can't get enough of them. Classic cucumber pickles are by far my favorite; I serve them in my Chile Bacon Bloody Mary and straight from the jar during most of my cocktail parties. No need to waste money on store-bought pickles any more—once you try these, you'll be hooked.

▶ MAKES 1 QUART (960 ML) ◀

Heat a medium saucepan over medium heat. Add the pickling spice and two of the árbol chiles and toast for 3 minutes, or until fragrant. Add the white vinegar, white wine vinegar, sugar, and salt, increase the heat to high, and bring them to a boil. Reduce the heat to low and simmer for 5 minutes, then add ½ cup (120 ml) water, return it to a simmer, and simmer for another 5 minutes. Turn off the heat and let it cool for 5 minutes. Place the cucumbers, dill, garlic, and the remaining 3 árbol chiles into a 1-quart (960-ml) Mason jar and strain the pickling liquid into the jar. Discard the pickling spice and 2 toasted árbol chiles. Let the pickles cool, then cover and refrigerate them for 24 hours before serving. The pickles will keep in an airtight container in the refrigerator for up to 2 weeks.

Pickled Cantaloupe

2 tablespoons pickling spice

3 star anise pods

1½ cups (360 ml) rice vinegar

¼ cup (50 g) granulated sugar

2 tablespoons salt

1 small cantaloupe (about 2½ pounds/1.2 kg), cut in half, seeds scooped out, and cubed

1 medium fennel bulb, top trimmed and thinly sliced

3 tablespoons chopped fennel fronds

Pickles make the perfect snack, and pickling adds big, bold flavor to even the mildest of foods, like the cantaloupe in this recipe. I love how the cantaloupe picks up the flavor of the pickling liquid and hints of the fennel. Try these pickles as I have presented at first, and then go crazy with pickle flavors of your own creation. If history has taught us anything in the food world, it's that damn near anything can be pickled.

▬▬▬➡ MAKES 1 QUART (960 ML) ⬅▬▬▬

Heat a medium saucepan over medium heat. Add the pickling spice and star anise and toast for 3 minutes, or until fragrant. Add the vinegar, sugar, and salt, increase the heat to high, and bring them to a boil. Reduce the heat to low and simmer for 5 minutes, then add ½ cup (120 ml) water, return it to a simmer, and simmer for another 5 minutes. Turn off the heat and let it cool for 5 minutes. Place the cantaloupe, fennel, and fennel fronds in alternating layers into a 1-quart (960-ml) Mason jar (if you have more cantaloupe than can fit in the jar, eat it as a cook's snack) and strain the pickling liquid into the jar. Discard the pickling spice and star anise. Let the pickles cool, then cover and refrigerate them for 24 hours before serving. The pickles will keep in an airtight container in the refrigerator for up to 1 week.

Roasted Garlic and Citrus Olives

1   small orange, zest julienned

¼   cup (60 ml) extra-virgin olive oil

1   tablespoon sherry vinegar

1   tablespoon fresh lemon juice

8   cloves Roasted Garlic (page 16)

1   tablespoon honey

1   teaspoon Maldon sea salt

½   teaspoon freshly ground black pepper

8   ounces (225 g) kalamata olives (with pits)

8   ounces (225 g) whole Queen or other green olives (with pits)

When roasted, garlic becomes quite sweet and works in tandem with the citrus to marinate these olives. Olives are one of the world's great bar snacks, so I always try to have some out when having friends over for cocktails. These olives are very fast to put together, but they do need twenty-four hours to marinate, so start them a day ahead of your next party. Whip them up and watch them disappear.

MAKES ABOUT 1 QUART (960 ML)

Squeeze 3 tablespoons of juice from the orange and use the rest for another purpose (like to make the orange-saffron reduction for my Chilean Sea Bass on page 85). In a large bowl, combine the oil, vinegar, orange juice, lemon juice, roasted garlic, honey, salt, and pepper and whisk to dissolve the honey and break up the garlic. Add the olives and orange zest and mix well to coat them. Transfer them to an airtight container and refrigerate them for at least 24 hours and up to 1 week to marinate. Remove from the refrigerator and let them come to room temperature before serving. The marinated olives will keep for about 1 week in the refrigerator.

Spicy Garlic Chicken Wings

with Blue Cheese Dipping Sauce

When it's wings night, this is the dish my friends will ask me for. It's fairly easy to put together, and it's one of the few recipes that you will find me using minced garlic from a jar; that's because the uniform size of the jarred garlic makes for the most successful frying, and the crispy garlic bits are what really set these wings apart. I prefer using Texas Pete hot sauce for this recipe, as I find it works best with the garlic and gives the wings a very familiar flavor set against this new, modern spin. I am not a fan of battered wings, so to get these wings crisp all over, I use a double-frying technique: cooking the wings through the first round, then frying them until crisp on the second run through.

▬▬▬▶ SERVES 8 TO 10 ◀▬▬▬

Make the blue cheese dipping sauce: In a medium bowl, combine the mayonnaise, blue cheese, sour cream, heavy cream, Worcestershire sauce, and lemon juice and season with salt and pepper. Stir well with a fork to break down any large chunks of blue cheese; cover and refrigerate for at least 1 hour for the flavors to come together. The dipping sauce will last for up to 1 week in an airtight container.

Fry the garlic: Measure out 2 tablespoons of the minced garlic and set it aside for the wing sauce. Drain the remaining minced garlic from the jar and spread it onto a paper towel–lined plate in an even layer. Place another paper towel on top of the garlic and allow it to sit for 20 minutes to remove as much moisture as possible.

(recipe continues)

FOR THE BLUE CHEESE DIPPING SAUCE:

- 1 cup (240 ml) mayonnaise
- 5 ounces (140 g) good-quality blue cheese, crumbled
- ¼ cup (60 ml) sour cream
- 2 tablespoons heavy cream
- 1 tablespoon Worcestershire sauce
- 2 tablespoons fresh lemon juice

Salt and lots of freshly ground black pepper

FOR THE FRIED GARLIC AND WINGS:

- 1 (4½-ounce/130-g) jar minced garlic

2 to 3 quarts (2 to 2.8 L) peanut oil

- 4 pounds (1.8 kg) small to medium chicken wings

Salt and freshly ground black pepper

FOR THE WING SAUCE:

- 1½ cups (360 ml) Texas Pete hot sauce
- 1 fresh cayenne or habanero chile, cut in half
- 2 tablespoons honey
- 1 tablespoon white wine vinegar
- ½ stick (2 ounces/55 g) cold unsalted butter

Salt and freshly ground black pepper

Chile-Bacon Bloody Mary, page 191, *and* Spicy Garlic Chicken Wings, opposite

While the garlic is sitting, heat the oil over medium heat to 350°F (175°C) in a deep fryer or large, heavy-bottomed pot, preferably cast iron.

Place the garlic in a small fine-mesh strainer and slowly lower the strainer into the oil, making sure the garlic doesn't float out. Fry for about 1 minute, until golden brown, then remove the garlic to a new paper towel–lined plate to dry. (If any garlic did float out into the oil, scoop it up with the strainer so you don't wind up with burnt garlic in your oil.) Set it aside for plating and return the oil to 350°F (175°C) for frying the wings.

Prep the wings: Spread the chicken wings out on a wire rack set over a baking sheet. Season them with salt and allow the wings to sit for 30 minutes so the salt can extract some of their moisture and the wings can come to room temperature.

Make the wing sauce: While the wings are coming to room temperature, combine the hot sauce and ½ cup (120 ml) water in a large, heavy-bottomed skillet. Place them over medium-high heat, bring them to a simmer, and cook for 5 minutes. Add the chile, the reserved 2 tablespoons garlic, the honey, and

vinegar. Reduce the heat to medium and cook for 15 minutes, or until the sauce thickens a bit. Remove from the heat and whisk in the butter 1 tablespoon at a time. Season with salt and pepper. Set the sauce aside for finishing the wings, stirring occasionally. If the sauce thickens too much, stir in a little water.

Fry the wings: Preheat the oven to 200°F (90°C).

Using a slotted spoon, lower 8 to 10 wings into the oil and fry them for 10 minutes. Remove the wings to a clean wire rack set over a baking sheet and allow the oil to return to 350°F (175°C). Return the wings to the oil and fry them until crisp, 4 to 5 minutes, then return the wings to the wire rack and immediately season them with salt and pepper. Put them in the oven to keep warm and repeat with the remaining wings.

To serve: When all the wings have been fried, place them in a very large bowl, add the wing sauce, and toss well to coat. Toss in the fried garlic, saving some to sprinkle on top. Spread them on a large platter with the blue cheese dipping sauce on the side and the remaining fried garlic sprinkled on top.

Sweet and Spicy Beef Jerky

2 pounds (910 g) flank steak, excess fat trimmed

¼ cup (55 g) packed brown sugar

1 teaspoon red pepper flakes

1 teaspoon garlic powder

1 teaspoon onion powder

¼ cup (60 ml) soy sauce

2 tablespoons Worcestershire sauce

1 tablespoon hoisin sauce

1 tablespoon ponzu sauce

1 tablespoon sambal oelek (chili-garlic paste)

1 tablespoon fresh lime juice

Whenever I go on a road trip, beef jerky is my gas station snack of choice, and it makes a great salty bar snack when having a few beers with friends. Making your own beef jerky is surprisingly easy and gives you the option of trying out any flavor combination you like. I use my dehydrator for this recipe, but you can also make it in the oven at the lowest setting. Make this jerky for your next road trip or to share over beers in the backyard with friends.

▬▶ MAKES ABOUT 1 POUND (455 G) ◀▬

Freeze the steak for 1 hour (this will make slicing it easier), then thinly slice into ¼-inch strips. Place the steak in a large zip-top bag. In a small bowl, whisk together the sugar, red pepper flakes, garlic powder, onion powder, soy sauce, Worcestershire sauce, hoisin sauce, ponzu sauce, sambal oelek, and lime juice well to dissolve the sugar. Pour the marinade over the steak, seal the bag, and gently massage the marinade into the meat. Refrigerate it for at least 24 hours and up to 2 days.

If you are using a dehydrator, remove the steak slices from the marinade and spread them out on the racks of a dehydrator without touching and dehydrate them at 155°F (68°C) for about 3 hours, until dried.

If using your oven, preheat it to 170°F (70°C) if it goes that low; if not, set it to 200°F (90°C). Spread the steak slices out without touching on wire racks placed over baking sheets. Bake them for about 2½ hours (or 2 hours at 200°F/90°C), until dried. Let them cool and store the jerky in an airtight container for up to 2 weeks, but I guarantee they won't last that long.

Spicy Garlic Head-On Shrimp

1 pound (455 g) large head-on shrimp

2 tablespoons extra-virgin olive oil

1 ounce (28 g) cured Spanish chorizo, finely diced

1½ tablespoons Chile-Lime Butter (page 18)

Salt and freshly ground black pepper

½ teaspoon ground cayenne

3 dried árbol chiles, toasted (see page 16), stemmed, and crumbled

8 cloves garlic, minced

1½ tablespoons fresh lemon juice

Roughly chopped fresh flat-leaf parsley

I know it seems like I have a lot of "spicy garlic" recipes in my book, but hey, why not—it's a perfect flavor combination. For this recipe, I looked to Spain and the famous tapas dish *gambas al ajillo*, which essentially translates to "shrimp in garlic." Don't be put off by the amount of garlic in this recipe; it doesn't overpower the other flavors and works great with the spicy chiles and smoky Spanish chorizo. If you can't find head-on shrimp, headless shrimp will work just fine. You will likely need to cook the shrimp in batches; add a portion of the flavoring ingredients to each batch.

SERVES 2 TO 4

To clean the shrimp, take a pair of kitchen shears and, starting right behind the head, cut down the shell to the tail without removing the shell. Using a paring knife, remove the intestinal tract of the shrimp under running water, working carefully so as not to tear off the shell.

In a large cast-iron skillet, heat the oil over medium-high heat until almost smoking. Add the chorizo and cook for 3 minutes, or until starting to brown. Add the chile-lime butter and cook until melted and bubbling. Add the shrimp in a single layer and season with salt and pepper and half of the cayenne. Sprinkle the árbol chiles and garlic into the spaces between the shrimp so it can sizzle in the oil. Cook for about 2 minutes, tilting the pan and basting with the butter, until the shrimp are lightly colored on the bottom. Flip the shrimp, season them with more salt and pepper and the remaining cayenne, and cook for about 2 more minutes, continuing to tilt the pan and baste, until the shrimp begin to pull away from the shells. Transfer the shrimp to either a large serving bowl or several small individual bowls. Pour the butter, garlic, chorizo, and chiles from the pan over the shrimp. Pour the lemon juice over the shrimp, sprinkle with parsley, and serve.

Chile-Bacon Bloody Mary

With the American craft cocktail explosion, flavored or infused liquors are hitting the bar scene big time. Unfortunately, the liquor often contains artificial additives and rarely tastes like the real thing. So I started infusing my own liquor, and nowadays more often than not you'll find large Mason jars lining my counter with my newest concoctions. This chile-bacon infused vodka is one of my favorites and is absolutely perfect in a Bloody Mary. Since the chile and bacon make a strong flavor statement, you don't need to bring out the priciest vodka here; any mid-range brand will work. The recipe makes extra infused vodka for multiple Bloody Marys. The bacon-flavored rimming salt can be found in some grocery stores and liquor stores.

▶ **SERVES 2** ◀

Make the chile-bacon–infused vodka: Place the chiles and the bacon in a large jar, pour in the vodka, and seal the jar. Place it in a cool, dark area to infuse for 3 days, shaking the jar once a day. Pour the infused vodka through a strainer lined with a coffee filter into a jar (keep it tightly sealed in the pantry for up to 1 month).

Make the chile-bacon Bloody Mary: In a cocktail shaker, combine the infused vodka, Worcestershire sauce, steak sauce, lemon juice, lime juice, olive brine, pepper, and Bloody Mary mix and shake to combine well.

To garnish: Spread a little bacon-flavored salt onto a small plate for rimming the glasses. Pour the lemon juice onto a separate small plate. Dip the rim of each glass into the lemon juice, then into the bacon salt. Fill the glasses with ice and pour in the Bloody Marys. Set a strip of bacon, a celery stalk, a pickle wedge, and an olive into each drink and serve.

FOR THE CHILE-BACON–INFUSED VODKA:

- 5 fresh red Fresno or other red chiles, roughly chopped
- 2 strips bacon, cooked until crisp
- 2 cups (480 ml) vodka

FOR THE CHILE-BACON BLOODY MARY:

- 3 ounces (90 ml) chile-bacon–infused vodka (see above)
- 1½ tablespoons Worcestershire sauce
- 1 teaspoon A.1. steak sauce
- 2 teaspoons fresh lemon juice
- 2 teaspoons fresh lime juice
- 1 teaspoon olive brine
- 1 teaspoon freshly ground black pepper
- 8 ounces (240 ml) premium Bloody Mary mix

FOR THE GARNISHES:

Bacon-flavored salt
- 2 tablespoons fresh lemon juice
Ice cubes
- 2 strips bacon, cooked until crisp
- 2 small stalks celery
- 2 dill pickle wedges
- 2 large green olives

Burnt Blue Rosemary Gin Smash

Several years ago, I decided to plant some rosemary; unlike the rest of my garden, it has no problems growing in the desert. So with an abundance of rosemary on hand, I decided to start testing it out in cocktails, and that's how this one was born. Even though I am not a big fan of gin, this drink is now a favorite on my cocktail menu when I throw dinners for my friends and family. The blueberry syrup makes enough for a second round of cocktails.

➡ SERVES 2 ⬅

Make the blueberry syrup: In a small saucepan, combine the blueberries, ¼ cup (60 ml) water, and the sugar. Place it over medium heat and bring the ingredients to a simmer, then reduce the heat to low and simmer for 10 minutes to dissolve the sugar and break down the blueberries. Remove from the heat and strain the syrup into a bowl, pressing on the berries with a spoon to squeeze out their juices. Let it cool.

Make the cocktails: In a cocktail shaker, combine the blueberries, rosemary, lemon juice, and 2 tablespoons blueberry syrup and muddle. Add the gin, cover, and shake well. Double strain the cocktail into two rocks glasses filled with ice and top each with a splash of club soda.

Using a culinary torch, singe the lemon peel twists. Garnish each cocktail with three blueberries, a sprig of rosemary, and a burnt lemon twist.

FOR THE BLUEBERRY SYRUP:

¼ cup (35 g) fresh blueberries

¼ cup (50 g) pure cane sugar

FOR THE BURNT BLUE ROSEMARY GIN SMASH:

2 tablespoons fresh blueberries

2 sprigs fresh rosemary

2 tablespoons fresh lemon juice

2 tablespoons blueberry simple syrup (see above)

4 ounces (120 ml) good-quality gin

Ice cubes

Couple of splashes of club soda

FOR THE GARNISHES:

2 lemon peel twists

6 fresh blueberries

2 sprigs fresh rosemary

A Manhattan in Vegas

2 ounces (60 ml) sweet vermouth, preferably Antica

8 fresh blueberries

4 ounces (120 ml) Bulleit Bourbon

3 dashes Peychaud's Bitters

Ice cubes

2 bamboo skewers, each speared with 5 blueberries

Manhattan aficionados probably will not like this recipe. To make a proper Manhattan, you must follow the rules of the drink, but since I have never been one to follow the rules, I am going to mess with this drink and make it my own. To be honest, I've made only one main change from the classic—muddling blueberries into the mix and garnishing the cocktail with blueberry skewers—but this blueberry-spiked Vegas Manhattan is so tasty that I'd wager any Manhattan aficionado open-minded enough to try it would agree!

SERVES 2

Combine the vermouth with the blueberries in a cocktail shaker and muddle them lightly. Add the bourbon and bitters, fill the cocktail shaker with ice, and stir until cold (do not shake). Strain the cocktails into chilled martini glasses and garnish each with a blueberry skewer.

Basil Basil Bourbon Berry

I created this cocktail with my good friends Ryan and Chuck, and it's absolutely perfect on a hot summer day. The blackberries and basil give it a freshness that is quite unexpected from a bourbon drink and a unique flavor experience not often found behind the bar. I use Basil Hayden's bourbon for this drink, but any high-quality bourbon can be used. The blackberry syrup makes enough for a second round of cocktails.

SERVES 2

Make the blackberry syrup: In a very small saucepan, combine the blackberries, ¼ cup (60 ml) water, and the sugar. Place it over medium heat and bring the ingredients to a simmer, then reduce the heat to low and simmer for 10 minutes to dissolve the sugar and break down the berries a little. Remove from the heat and strain the syrup into a cup, pressing on the berries with a spoon to squeeze out their juices. Let it cool.

Make the cocktails: In a cocktail shaker, combine the lemon juice, basil leaves, blackberries, and 2 tablespoons blackberry syrup and muddle them. Add the bourbon, cover, and shake well. Fill two tall glasses with ice, strain the drink into the glasses, and top each with a splash of club soda. Garnish each cocktail with a blackberry and a basil leaf.

FOR THE BLACKBERRY SYRUP:

8   fresh blackberries

¼   cup (50 g) pure cane sugar

FOR THE BASIL BASIL BOURBON BERRY:

2   tablespoons fresh lemon juice

5   fresh basil leaves

6   fresh blackberries

2   tablespoons blackberry syrup (see above)

4   ounces (120 ml) Basil Hayden's bourbon

Ice cubes

Couple of splashes of club soda

FOR THE GARNISHES:

2   fresh blackberries

2   large fresh basil leaves

New Vegas Old Fashioned

6 fresh blackberries

4 sprigs fresh thyme

1½ ounces (45 ml) simple syrup (see Note)

Juice of ½ orange

3 ounces (90 ml) Bulleit Bourbon

2 dashes Angostura Bitters

1 dried árbol chile, toasted (see page 16), stemmed, and broken into pieces

Ice cubes

2 orange peel twists

I am absolutely, positively a whiskey and bourbon man through and through! At the majority of clubs and pools where I DJ, I don't even have to order anymore. I walk into the DJ booth and my Jack Daniel's Single Barrel is on the way, and if the Single Barrel is unavailable, it's straight to the Bulleit Bourbon. Most of the time, I will drink these straight with one or two ice cubes, but recently my friends Ryan and Chuck have been working with me to bring bourbon into my cocktails. Here, we added a new spin to an old favorite to completely transform it. If you are a bourbon drinker, you are going to love this one!

SERVES 2

In a tall glass, muddle two of the blackberries with two sprigs of the thyme and the simple syrup. Add the orange juice, bourbon, bitters, and chile along with a scoop of ice and stir until cold. Using a culinary torch, singe the orange peel twists. Double strain the cocktails into two rocks glasses and garnish each glass with a burnt orange peel, a couple of remaining blackberries, and a sprig of fresh thyme.

Note: To make 1½ ounces (45 ml) simple syrup, in your smallest pan, combine 2½ tablespoons water and 2½ tablespoons granulated sugar. Place the pan over medium heat and stir until the sugar dissolves, then continue to simmer for another minute. Transfer the syrup to a bowl to cool completely before using.

Grapefruit, Cucumber, and Jalapeño Margarita

When I lived in Florida, citrus was everywhere. There was even a lime tree in my neighbor's yard, and we took full advantage of it, with fresh citrus margaritas becoming a pretty common cocktail on my party menus. This cocktail starts with the standard lime margarita base and then adds grapefruit, cucumber, and jalapeño to give a new spin on the classic.

→ **SERVES 2** ←

Make the margaritas: Combine the simple syrup, jalapeño, and cucumber in a cocktail shaker and muddle well. Add the tequila, triple sec, lime juice, and grapefruit juice. Fill the cocktail shaker with ice, cover, and shake well.

To garnish: Pour the lime juice onto a small plate and sprinkle some kosher salt onto another small plate. Rim two rocks glasses by dipping them first into the lime juice, then the salt. Fill the glasses with ice and strain the margarita into the glasses. Garnish by running a bamboo skewer through one side of a jalapeño strip and through a cucumber round lengthwise, then run the skewer through the other side of the jalapeño strip to create a half circle around the cucumber. Finish by placing a lime wedge at the end of the skewer. Repeat with a second skewer, set the skewers on the glasses, and serve.

FOR THE MARGARITAS:

- 1 ounce (30 ml) simple syrup (see Note, page 196)
- 3 (⅛-inch-/3-mm-thick) strips jalapeño chile
- 4 (⅛-inch-/3-mm-thick) cucumber rounds
- 3 ounces (90 ml) good-quality silver tequila
- 1½ ounces (45 ml) triple sec
- Juice of 2 limes
- Juice of ½ grapefruit
- Ice cubes

FOR THE GARNISHES:

- Juice of 1 lime
- Kosher salt
- 2 cucumber rounds
- 2 long jalapeño chile strips
- 2 lime wedges

Acknowledgments

First and foremost to my dad, I miss you every day! Thank you for always pushing me to pursue my dreams and for always encouraging me to give my best effort at whatever I do. You will continue to inspire me for the rest of my days.

To my mother, without you none of this is possible: the DJ career, the *MasterChef* title, none of this exists without your love and support! Thank you so much for being you. I strive every day to make you proud to call me son.

To my best friend, Ryan Lee, my sister-in-law, Aida Lee, and my godson, Marco Lee. Ryan, you are the best friend I have ever had and could ever ask for. This life would not be the same without you as my right-hand man. Thank you from the bottom of my heart for being with me through all of the ups and downs. Aida, I couldn't be happier to have you in my life and could not imagine it without you! The joy you brought to Ryan's life overflows to me and I am proud to call you sister whether legally related or not. To my godson, Marco "Spartacus" Lee, I hope my experiences in life, whether good or bad, encourage you to always follow your dreams. No one can stop you when you set your mind to a goal and attack relentlessly! Nothing in this world will be given to you but with hard work and determination you can achieve whatever your heart desires.

To my brother, Tim, I know we have not always had the best of relationships but I treasure the time we now spend together. The word *step* does not cross my mind when calling you my brother. To my nephew, TJ, find what you are passionate about and don't look back. Your life is just beginning; get out there and make the most of it!

To Chuck—you have been one of my closest friends for as long as I can remember. Without your support in the kitchen and with the dishes, I don't know if I could have pulled this off.

A very special thank-you to Gordon Ramsay and Christina Tosi for pushing me and inspiring me every day in the *MasterChef* Kitchen. It was such an honor to cook for you and learn from you. Also, a very big thank-you to all of the incredible guest judges—it was truly humbling cooking for you all, so thank you to Aarón Sánchez, Edward Lee, Kevin Sbraga, Richard Blais, Wolfgang Puck, and Daniel Boulud. I am still in shock that I had the opportunity to cook for this list of culinary legends!

To my friends, DJ Que, I can't thank you enough for joining Ryan and me on that amazing trip to Italy. You are an amazing person and I am proud to call you friend. DJ Earwaxxx, thank you for your continued support. I can't wait to get back to work in the DJ booth with you. Mikee, you have had my back for a long time, brother. Thank you so much for being there for me no matter what the situation. Ryan McViety, I wish I had the chance to see you more often, man. You have always been one of my best friends and I miss sharing these crazy experiences with you. Steven and Jenny, thanks for always being there to party it up with me—glad we have become friends over the years. Donna and Robert Lee, thank you so much for treating me like your own. I hope I have made you proud. Regis Gillespie and Pearce Cleveland, thank you both for the amazing opportunities you have given me in the DJ world in Tampa and Las Vegas. You have both become dear friends. Josh Sorensen, thank you for everything you did for my father and for becoming a dear friend. Steve Cunningham, I can't tell you how much it means to me that you took the time off to attend the *MasterChef* Finale. Your presence truly made me feel as though my dad was there, too.

A big thank-you for the constant support, whether in the DJ booth or in the kitchen, to

Katie Provost, Josh Ouzer, Travis Crow, Gideon Vandegrift, Bobby Debaise, Matt Chandler, Elisa Freitas, Kyle Heverly, Jenny Gonzalez, Dianne Bizzaro, Ben Lugar, Chris and Joey, Kalika Moquin, Jennifer Wieder, Carl White, Jeremy Schlader and family, Mike Ross, Will Quinn, Merri Jo and Mike, Rob McGreuder and Rachel Orsini, Lisette Barajas, Marcelle, Rob Klimp, The Hardnox, Neal Harris and Francesca, Luis Eshgy, Dillon Francis, George Acosta, DJ X, DJ Direct, and Dee Spuriel.

To my *MasterChef* family: I love you all. You have become so dear to me and I am so honored to have shared this unique experience with each and every one of you. Brandi Mudd, you are one of my best friends! Who knew the schoolteacher and the DJ would have such a unique bond? Thank you for sharing your recipe with me. Alejandro Toro, I am so happy this experience brought your friendship into my life. You and your story are truly inspiring. Andrea Galan, I love ya, little sister. Eric Howard and Manny Washington, I'm proud to call you both friends. Thank you for your service. Lisa Ann, you are amazing—thank you for all your encouragement. Nathan, I am so proud of you, my friend. David, I know we had our moments, but it was an honor to cook with you. Katie, you are such a strong person. It was inspiring to watch you battle. Terry, the man with the magic hands, it was a pleasure to cook with you. Wild Bill, I love you, buddy, so glad we have become friends. You, Ashley, and Myles have become like family. To our beauty queen, Diamond, your future holds big things, my dear. Dan, your growth on the show was inspiring to watch. Tannoria, Cassie, Diana, and Barbara—it was a blast cooking with you. D'Andre and Brittany, thank you so much for all of your help in the kitchen. You two have become very dear to me and I don't know how I could pull off some of these parties without you. To the remaining *MasterChef* family, I love you all. I know I am forgetting some of you and I truly hope you know how much you all mean to me whether top 20, top 40, or top 80, and all the way to all of you who auditioned around the country.

A huge thanks to Robin, Yasmin, Adeline, and the entire production team for continuing to make home cooks' dreams come true. Thank you for seeing something in me that I was hiding.

Another huge thank-you to Avery, Ben, Mary, and the amazing culinary crew—you guys are hands down the best team in food television, and without you the show would not be what it is.

Thank you to Ana, Brian, Tommy, Felipe, Candace, Gina, Patrick, Brady, Spencer, and everyone else behind the cameras on the production crew. The work you do is beautiful and dramatic. This season of *MasterChef* looked amazing!

To those who kept us safe and sound: JP, Kris, Tony, Mikey, Kit, Lamar, Ryan, and everybody else in casting, thank you for keeping my head on my shoulders and talking me through the times of doubt I had throughout the whole process! You guys are underappreciated but please know that I thank you for all of your sacrifices.

To the team at Endemol Shine, thank you for all of the amazing opportunities. Vivi, Thomas, Joe, Julie, Marissa, Rob, Jaycee, and the countless others—none of this would be possible without you; thank you for all you have done to make dreams reality.

Thank you to Holly Dolce, Danielle Young, Mary O'Mara, and Sarah Massey, the amazing team from Abrams who brought my vision to life in the pages of this book. To my amazing photography team, Andrew Purcell, Carrie Purcell, and Kate Prop, words cannot express how grateful I am for your hard work, the photos in this book are truly something special!

Thank you to Leda Scheintaub and Patricia Austin for helping me write one amazing cookbook. You were both a pleasure to work with and I couldn't have done it without you.

Finally, thank you to my management team, Blueprint Sound, for all of your continued hard work, and the city of Las Vegas for the love and support.

Index